From V̶
Westminster

The Story of
Dr. Martyn Lloyd-Jones

told by
his grandson

Christopher Catherwood

Acknowledgements

As always, I am deeply grateful to my publishers at Christian Focus, who have been wonderfully patient in waiting for this manuscript to arrive.

I am equally indebted to my wonderful wife, Paulette, who, as well as helping to ensure that this manuscript was written, read through everything very carefully and was, as ever, of inestimable help in the whole process.

Lastly, many thanks must be given to the many people at Cambridge who provided enough teaching jobs for me to live off this past year, while putting this and other books together.

Cambridge
March 1998

Dedication

To the memory of
Martyn Lloyd-Jones,
and to *Paulette*, my wife.

IMPORTANT NOTE

The dialogue in this book, put in at the publisher's request,
is my own invention. I trust, though, that it is the kind
of dialogue which Martyn Lloyd-Jones would have used.
If reading this book helps you to go on and read what he
actually said and wrote, so much the better!

Copyright © 1999 Christopher Catherwood
Reprinted 2000 and 2005

ISBN 185792 349 9

Published by
Christian Focus Publications Ltd,
Geanies House, Fearn, Tain, Ross-shire
IV20 1TW, Scotland, Great Britain

Cover Illustration by Neil Reed

Printed and bound in Denmark
by Nørhaven Paperback A/S

Contents

'I remember, about a year after we moved to Llangeitho, as I was playing with a number of children outside the school, that I begged them not to speak English to me any more, 'Speak Welsh to me - I'm a Welshman now!'

Martyn Lloyd-Jones

'Salvation does not erase natural and national characteristics. It is the man or the soul which is re-born and not his characteristics, his abilities, or his temperament. The gospel does not produce a number of people who are exactly the same as one another like postage stamps.'

Martyn Lloyd-Jones

Fire in Llangeitho

'Fire! Fire!' A woman's voice was heard to shout frantically. Instantly men, women and children, were all up and out of their beds, staring out of the windows at the smoke that was seeping from every nook and cranny of the General Store.

Workmen struggled on with their boots while their wives rushed to organize buckets. Hopefully the family were out by now. It wouldn't take long for that fire to get going. There was a fierce wind tonight and once a fire had the wind to fan it along the whole store would burn to a crisp.

However, as the villagers frantically organised fire fighting equipment, the Lloyd-Jones family, sound asleep in their beds, were blissfully ignorant that their family home and livelihood was just about to go up in smoke. The flames spread rapidly through the house in the pretty little Welsh village of Llangeitho. Smoke curled its way up the stairs to the bedrooms where the Lloyd-Jones continued to sleep. Two boys, Martyn, aged ten, and Vincent, nearly eight, gently snored, curled up under their covers.

Martyn half woke. His throat was a bit sore and his eyes were stinging. 'Bit of a stink, Vincent,' he groaned to his brother, as the powerful smell of the smoke wafted into their small bedroom. Vincent nodded. The two boys pulled the sheets over their heads and went back to sleep. Neither of them had twigged what the smell was and as they fell back to sleep they fell back into danger. The pungent smell which had briefly woken Martyn was that of the fumes of the now raging fire. The heat was so intense that downstairs their father's gold sovereigns were melted together in the sheer heat of the flames. Their father Henry, a man with a wonderful walrus moustache, was asleep nearby. As he was the village shopkeeper, it was his general store that was now ablaze. And it was his general store that the local families were now desperately trying to save.

'Surely they can't be sleeping through this lot?' someone yelled.

'Well, it wouldn't surprise me if that Henry Lloyd-Jones slept through a herd of elephants charging through Llangeitho! Wake up man! Your lives are in danger! Get out now while you can!' The local milliner banged his fists in desperation on the door, for Henry was a heavy sleeper. Smoke was coming out everywhere and people were beginning to cough as the fumes attacked their lungs.

'Wake up Mr. Lloyd-Jones! Wake up or you'll all die!'

It was 1 o'clock in the morning of January 20th, 1910 and it was bitterly cold. Other villagers affected by the fire had escaped long since but Mr. Lloyd-Jones and his two sons were still inside.

Three men, wearing just their long night-shirts, were shivering out in the road, having already escaped. Mrs. Magdalen Lloyd-Jones, a local farmer's daughter, and Harold, the eldest boy, were ushered away by friends and neighbours to safety having eventually made it out of the burning store alive. Slowly Henry emerged. His face was as white as a sheet as he stared at what was his whole life going up in flames.

'Fire! The shop!' His voice was hoarse and he could hardly get the words out. Then he realized, 'The boys, my sons. They are still inside.'

He had to rescue the boys. Braving the smoke and flames, he rushed back into the burning store and found his way through the flames and the smoke to Martyn and Vincent's bedroom.

Coughing and spluttering he pulled the blankets off the two sleepy boys. They were already beginning to suffer the effects of smoke inhalation.

With one heave he pulled both of the boys out of their beds. Holding Vincent in one arm and Martyn in the other he made his way to the window. Quickly he placed Vincent down by the window and after a brief struggle with the latch he let the fresh air into the bedroom.

Both Vincent and Martyn gulped in the clean, fresh air. Quickly Henry hurled Martyn out of the window, into safety and into the arms of a man waiting below in the street, Vincent soon followed.

A friend rushed to the scene with a ladder. Henry and little Vincent clambered down, just in time. The fresh air let in by the open window was refanning the flames and giving new life to the already blazing inferno. The three of them were rescued, alive, though the shop was an absolute ruin. Neighbours rushed to help the brave father get his children away from the awful sight of their home being burnt to the ground. Comforting arms patted the ex-Llangeitho store owner on the back and sympathetic eyes looked into his, expressing sympathy at his loss, but also relief that this time it hadn't been their homes.

The following morning, as the ashes cooled and the cold light of day showed the family just what a narrow escape they'd had, they searched for items they might be able to rescue or salvage.

The melted sovereigns - which were virtually useless and a cracked and discoloured mug were all that was left of the Llangeitho general store. Apart from the clothes they stood up in the Lloyd-Jones family had absolutely nothing to call their own. The fire, for this closely-knit family, was a financial disaster. But on the other hand, they had experienced a mighty deliverance. God had been watching over them that night. They had all escaped with their lives.

Martyn, the little boy rescued that stormy January night, would speak of his experiences many years later.

'Somehow things at Llangeitho were never the same after the fire. Although we built a new home, and started living in it within the year, things were different. Certainly as a building the new house was a great improvement on our former home, but there was something missing, and more than anything the feeling of home was lacking. I felt as if I were in a strange house and that living there was a temporary matter.'

It was a big trauma for a young child, and one that stayed with him for the rest of his life.

If the milliner's fists had not been loud enough, or if Henry had not been brave enough to rescue his sons, Martyn and his younger brother would not have lived. Nor would you be reading this book! Because I am Martyn's grandson, his daughter's son, and the author of the biography you are looking at today. God had preserved Martyn's life and done so for a great purpose. For the ten-year-old saved that cold January night was to go on to have a career that influenced millions of people all over the world. Indeed, Martyn Lloyd-Jones continues to influence people many years after his death, aged eighty-one, seventy-one years after the fire of Llangeitho.

'Somehow things at Llangeitho were never the same after the fire. Although we built a new home and started living in it within the year things were different. Certainly as a building the new house was a great improvement on our former home, but there was something missing, and more than anything the feeling of home was lacking. I felt as if I were in a strange house and that living there was a temporary matter.'

Martyn Lloyd-Jones

Early Days

Martyn Lloyd-Jones was born on December 20th, 1899, the middle son of Henry Lloyd-Jones, a storekeeper and his wife Magdalen, the daughter of David Evans, a prosperous farmer. Martyn was therefore always the same age as the century except for 11 days.

Nowadays, with more opportunities, Henry would have been a professor. But back then things were very different and instead he ended up a store keeper - a worthy profession and one which provided for his family until the disastrous fire.

Henry was a gentle, quiet, kindly, bookish man who loved to read. In fact there was nothing he enjoyed more than the simple pleasure of sitting down with a book, by the fire for a good read. Martyn however didn't really take to books and much preferred to play football with the other boys. Kicking a ball around was much more fun than having your head stuck in a book. However, Martyn's aversion to books and learning would one day change for good.

The Evans side of the family, Henry Lloyd-Jones' in-laws, were the go-getters in Martyn's family. Martyn's Mother had been an Evans before she married Henry. They were successful and moderately ambitious. Old Evans, Martyn's grandfather, had a farm, Llwyncadfor, which was actually as big as a small village.

It wasn't just any old farm but went by the grand title of 'Stud Farm'. That meant that it was a farm for breeding horses and Martyn's grandfather was an expert horse breeder. Welsh cobs, shire horses and hackneys were all found at Llwyncadfor and Martyn loved to spend his Summer holidays helping groom and care for them.

Each horse had its own individual box and very often the Llwyncadfor Stud Farm would walk off with all the best rosettes and prizes at the Welsh agricultural fairs.

There was one horse in particular, its name was 'Model' because it was a model horse. Martyn was really proud of 'Model' as every prize that this horse won was a first prize. When a Llwyncadfor horse won a prize Martyn's heart would fill with pride. What the Evans family didn't know about horses wasn't worth knowing.

Sometimes the whole stud farm would up sticks and leave for an agricultural show somewhere. On occasions such as these the Llwyncadfor stud farm would commandeer an entire train just for themselves and their animals.

Now and then Martyn would be allowed to lead one of the more gentle horses all the way to the loading bay at the station. Even with a gentle animal it was quite a responsibility and Martyn was thrilled that his grandfather trusted him enough to do this.

Martyn's grandfather was such a famous horse breeder people would actively seek him out. He was one of the best horse breeders around and if you were after a really good beast 'Old Evans' was the man to speak to. He was known all over the land. Some horses did so well at the agricultural fairs that a foreign King sent courtiers all the way to the little village in Wales to buy them.

In the end Model was sold for a colossal sum of 800 guineas to the Spanish Government. Martyn was sad to see him go - he was a magnificent horse. But 800 guineas! Grandfather had done well!

For years all that Martyn wanted to be was a groom. The fire however made Martyn think about a lot of things and one thing that changed was Martyn's carefree lifestyle. The fire brought poverty for the whole family and it also brought responsibility to Martyn. A lot changed for the Lloyd-Jones family.

One thing that Martyn quickly learned as he spent time around the stud farm was that you didn't cross 'Old Evans'. Martyn's grandfather's temper could be legendary and so was his love of drink.

Martyn and his family had moved near to Martyn's grandfather, to the village of Llangeitho, in 1905, when Martyn was just six years old. Sometimes 'Old Evans' was too drunk to drive the pony and trap back from the village to the farm. Young Martyn would then have to come to the rescue and take the horse's reins to drive his grandfather safely home.

One day, just after the fire, 'Old Evans' was drunk again. Martyn to the rescue! As the old man slurred his speech and let the pony and trap wander all over the road Martyn quickly took the reins and gently directed the horses back on course.

Grandfather and grandson rode along with the beat of the pony's hooves sounding out on the dirt track and the old grandfather mumbling something or other. 'Your father's out of money, Martyn,' the old man began.

'What's he saying?' thought Martyn, anxiously. 'Out of money? Is it the drink talking or is he telling the truth?' Eventually Martyn realized that his grandfather was telling the truth and that their whole family was in a very precarious situation.

Martyn didn't have much money himself, or understand it very well, but he knew that this situation was serious. He'd have to become serious too. He would have to save money and put aside his pocket money to help at home.

He realized that the much loved game of football, which he enjoyed far more than studying properly for school, might be a hindrance to his family's prospects. 'I'll never make the scholarship if I don't buckle down', thought Martyn. 'If I don't make the scholarship I can't expect my father to pay. We just don't have the money. If I don't make the scholarship then I won't get a good position and I'll be a burden on my family and a failure!' Martyn's grandfather, unwittingly, was the push Martyn had needed to focus his mind on achieving that scholarship.

Martyn's family would never be able to afford to send him to further education - winning a scholarship was his only chance if he wanted to get on in life. And getting on in life was one way to help his family get back on their feet once again.

Martyn thought about it and decided that he would have to ration his football games. He would have to stop spending his pennies on sweeties at the local shop. He would have to really work hard at his school lessons - and work he did.

***

Martyn was the middle of the three boys. Harold, the eldest, was tall, handsome and a poet. The youngest was Vincent. All three boys were very clever, and in Wales in those days, that was something to be proud of: no one was ashamed of having good brains in the little village.

Martyn was a character from a very early age. In fact, he was a mischief! Once, when Vincent was a little baby, the proud parents wanted a photo of their three boys. That was something to show off in the village. But the photographer had a terrible time. 'Martyn! Stop pinching little Vincent! Stop making him cry!' So while Harold behaved himself , Vincent cried throughout the whole experience and Martyn had an impish grin all over his face.

Martyn's grandfather was a bit of a terror and he terrified many of his farm workers. But he loved his family. Sometimes when he would doze off, someone would say, 'Martyn! The brush!' Martyn would tiptoe over and brush the old man's hair. No one else dared. What fun those days were. Good times with good friends. Happy, carefree, never dull. Martyn had a store of happy memories to look back on throughout the rest of his life.

'If you were to ask me to give a definition of a Christian I should say that he is the one who, since believing in Christ, feels himself to be the happiest man in the world and longs for everybody else to be equally happy!'

Martyn Lloyd-Jones on Psalm 34:8

'Before we deal with the position of those who are outside, let us first examine ourselves and make our confession. For every true revival in the world starts as a revival in the church, and revivals come to churches which realise their need and impotence and turn to God in prayer and forgiveness and for new strength.'

Martyn Lloyd-Jones on John 10:10

Llangeitho Memories

One thing that the village of Llangeitho had was lots of characters! There were people there who had real stories to tell. These men and women had lived all their lives in the Welsh village. None of them had travelled very far but they had all led interesting lives. It was exciting to hear about them.

In between Martyn's studies and all his other responsibilities Martyn would hang out in the village with his friends. Quite often he would meet up with all these old characters. They were amazing. Martyn and his young friends never tired of hearing about their antics or their stories.

***

'Come, Martyn! See 'the boot' spit!'

The village boys, Martyn included, loved to visit the village blacksmith. He wasn't just great at shoeing all the local horses (including the grand horses belonging to Martyn's grandfather, 'Old Evans'), but 'the boot' as he was nicknamed was the best spitter around! He chewed tobacco and would spit it out at great distances. Martyn and his friends loved to see how far each spit could go!

'Wow did you see that one! How many yards do you think he did that time?' Martyn and his friends would sit for hours watching spit after spit after spit. Each one was different and more elaborate than the last. Martyn described him as an 'artistic spitter'. And there was an art to spitting as 'the boot' managed to leave a perfect pattern of spit all over the floor before closing up for the night.

One day a farmer came in to see 'the boot' complaining that his daughter had failed her examinations again. 'She'll never get into the Tregaron Intermediate School at this rate. Her mother and I just don't know what to do! Every time she fails she fails on the same thing - Algebra! Now could you tell me, what is this algebra that the lass is always failing in?'

'The boot' leaned back in his chair and spat. 'Well man, it's like this. Think of a train that has just left the town of Aberystwyth with thirty passengers . It comes to Llanrhystyd and two get out and one steps in. At Llanilar, three get out and no one enters. Tregaron, five get off and six enter. Then from station to station until they arrive at Bronwydd Arms where twelve enter. At last the train reaches Carmarthen. Now this is the problem, - What was the guard's name?'

'No wonder the poor lass fails,' said the astonished farmer.

'The boot' was full of witty, discerning remarks and stories. He always knew exactly what to say.

***

Martyn also loved Rhys Rowlands, particularly his stories. It didn't matter what time of night he arrived at the Lloyd-Jones house Henry Lloyd-Jones would always trap him into telling a story - and the boys would sit and listen. A heavy smoker he would draw the smoke into his mouth then he would exhale the smoke with great gusto, waving the pipe erratically in the air at the same time. His stories would go on and on about minuscule details that bore no relation to the actual tale he was attempting to tell, but Rhys Rowlands was your man if you wanted to know local gossip, family news and any sort of general information spanning the entire county!

You'd mention that you'd seen Mr. Jones from Tregaron last week and away Rhys would go with a marathon story telling session.

'Well, I met that fellow three years back when I went to Tregaron on a Tuesday in February. I put the little yellow mare onto the trap - she's the foal of the old chestnut mare that we had for years and was sired by the hackney stallion 'Old Evans' had. Well I was driving the little yellow mare on the day that I met Mr. Jones from Tregaron and I remember as we drove the wind was that bitter and it was raining a cold drizzle, and then I met Gareth Davies, an old relative of mine on my mother's side. He's the one you know who married that girl from Carmarthen and she was the one whose mother went mad and threw the bed pan at her husband almost braining him and this all happened only the week before the wedding and we all thought the wedding might be off but the old man recovered and the whole show went on as if nothing had happened and he's doing quite well for himself apparently - no side effects at all…' There was no stopping the guy. You always felt ready for bed after Rhys Rowlands had been on one of his stories.

But there was always a sad air that surrounded old Rhys and Martyn knew why. There was another story - Rhys' own story of a broken heart.

Rhys had fallen deeply in love with a young woman he had met at Llanwrtyd Wells, on holiday one year. She was beautiful and sweet-natured and Rhys was stricken. They had spent a lot of time together - going on walks, laughing and joking the whole day long. Rhys had never enjoyed a holiday so much - he was so in love.

Waving goodbye to her at the station, Rhys felt that she was the one for him and was determined to keep in touch with her. He had said that he would write - only there was one problem. He couldn't write. He had never learned how. So he had to arrange some other way of keeping in touch. He asked his best friend, the local minister, to assist him. Rhys asked his friend to write to the beautiful young girl on his behalf and in his name. The minister did so; but after some time, and without Rhys' knowledge, the minister began to write on his own behalf instead. The story ended with the minister marrying the girl instead of Rhys.

Rhys' heart was broken. He felt betrayed and misused. Surely he had made himself a laughing stock. Rhys felt awful. But Rhys was of a very forgiving nature and his heartache didn't last too long.

The minister brought his new wife to the village and they lived happily ever after. Rhys forgave them both and no one in the whole chapel thought more highly of the minister than he did. Despite his friend's hurtful actions Rhys forgave him and continued their friendship. Both the minister and his wife were strong friends with Rhys for the rest of their lives.

When it was time for the minister to leave this world he actually died in the arms of Rhys Rowlands. 'It is quite incredible,' Martyn thought. 'Things always happen in the village and to the people who live in Llangeitho.'

Even just a simple errand could end up as an exciting, breath-taking adventure.

***

Martyn always remembered his first visit to London. Mr. Lloyd-Jones came in for tea one night and said 'Next week is the show at the Agricultural Hall in London. I can take one of the boys with me. Now which is it going to be?'

Both Martyn and his older brother Harold wanted to go. So to sort out the dispute it was decided they should draw lots. Two pieces of straw were chosen - one short, one long. Whoever drew the short straw stayed behind. If you drew the long straw then you were going to London!

The tension mounted as Harold went up to draw his straw. Martyn, watched, anxiously willing his brother to pick the short straw, which wasn't very nice of him but he was that desperate to go to London.

Harold's hand grasped a straw and he pulled. Martyn whooped! 'It's the short straw, the short straw! I'm going to London.'

Harold screwed up his face in annoyance and threw his piece of straw on the floor.

'Don't you mind son,' said Mr. Lloyd-Jones. 'There will be other shows and other trips to London.'

The following Monday, Martyn and his father packed up their belongings and left by train, expecting to return by train the following Saturday.

Martyn fairly enjoyed himself at the show. His father took him round one or two of the sights of London town in the evenings, before going back to their lodgings.

All too soon it was Friday evening and time to think about going back to Wales. Martyn and his father began to pack up their belongings once again. But just as they were packing their last bits and pieces into the case the landlady came up the stairs to talk to Mr. Lloyd-Jones.

'Sir, there's a gentleman to see you.' Henry Lloyd-Jones went down the stairs to see who it was.

'Why' he exclaimed. 'It's the squire himself. Welcome sir. What brings you here to London?'

'I've been doing some business in town and decided also to buy a car from a dealer while I was here. I heard you were here and wondered if you would like a lift back to Llangeitho tomorrow?'

'Why we would appreciate it sir, indeed. What time should we meet up?'

'Well, my lodgings aren't far. If we meet up at about 9 a.m. tomorrow you can come with me to choose the car and then we'll head off.'

Martyn's father looked a bit surprised. He had thought that the car was already purchased, but as it turned out it wasn't even chosen. Next morning Martyn and his father were to be found trekking round all the different garages of London looking at many different models of car. Cars from France, Germany, Italy and many other countries beside.

They had to wait for ages for the squire to make up his mind. This car was too expensive or not big enough, this other car did not have the right kind of roof, the next car was not the right colour. It was not an easy job. The squire could not make up his mind.

Time wore on and it was mid-afternoon. They arrived at a garage near King's Cross and the squire spotted a car that was just what he was looking for. It was an Italian model, a Darracq, built by Alpha Romeo. To say that it was in good nick would be a great exaggeration. It looked tired and second-hand.

Martyn looked on as the squire bargained with the owner of the garage and then signed a cheque for the amount. From behind him he heard some passers-by commenting on the condition of the car.

'I would not go fifty miles into the country in that car even supposing you paid me £50!'

Martyn turned round to see who was discussing the car. He felt a bit uneasy about this journey home now. Just then the squire and Martyn's father opened the boot and put in their luggage. Martyn ran up to his father just about to tell him what the people had been saying about the car when Mr. Lloyd-Jones said anxiously, 'Right Martyn, get in the back son and we'll soon be on our way. It's a bit of a drive and we don't want to be driving too late tonight.'

Martyn jumped in, deciding that it was too late now to tell the purchaser that some people thought his car was a wreck on wheels. He made a quick calculation. They had a journey of 300 miles ahead of them. Hopefully they'd be home for supper. But just out of the suburbs of London Martyn's hopes had a bit of a knock. Phizz… went a rear tyre. It was a puncture.

'Right then,' Martyn's father sighed. 'I'll get the spare tyre out of the boot. We'll soon be on our way.'

The squire looked sheepish. 'I'm afraid I bought the car without a spare tyre. I was planning to get a spare when we arrived back at Llangeitho.'

Martyn's father told him to head into a nearby hotel and keep warm by the fire while the squire and he repaired what was left of the burst tyre.

Later in the evening they resumed their journey but soon realized that punctures were going to be a common occurrence, so common in fact that they would have to be ignored if they were ever going to make it home to Wales at all.

The next stop was the following morning in the High Street of Oxford at 7a.m. when all four tyres were flat and in need of replacement!

The squire got out of the car and thumped the bonnet in frustration before dashing off to wake up the owner of a local cycle and tyre shop in the high street by the name of W. R. Morris.

Mr. Morris was overjoyed to get an order for four spanking new tyres. He hadn't had any business all week! The squire forked out for new tyres, and tubes and after breakfast at the Randolph hotel they were on their way again.

'Next stop Gloucester,' shouted the squire to Martyn as he lay crumpled up in the back seat of the car. None of them had managed to sleep a wink all night. They were all shattered.

Trundling along that Sunday morning the main problem was the extreme December cold. The car was entirely open to the elements. Martyn huddled on the floor to get some shelter. Everybody else sat and froze.

Abergavenny was reached in time for supper on Sunday evening but only after the car had managed to clamber up Brecon Road. Brecon Road being a really steep climb Martyn and his father had to walk up the hill. The car reached the summit where the squire waited for them to huff and pant their way up to the top! What a journey!

Regular telegrams along their journey had kept Mrs. Lloyd-Jones in touch with their progress and when at length they finally arrived at Llangeitho at about 9 p.m. on the Monday, the three very weary travellers were met by a crowd of villagers. They had driven without rest for two whole days, yet only once, when someone had fallen asleep at the wheel, had the vehicle left the road.

Everybody cheered when they got out of the car. Harold came and thumped Martyn on the back. The conquering heroes had returned. This was a story to be told at the warm, Llangeitho, firesides for quite a few weeks to come.

***

Martyn also loved going out in the pony and trap with his father. One day his father decided that he should pay a visit to two old bachelor farmers who lived about six miles outside the village of Llangeitho.

Martyn liked going to visit these two old farmers as they were another pair of characters and highly amusing. This visit proved to be just as amusing.

The two brothers were famous for disagreeing. The older one was conservative and disliked change. He was also the boss and his decision was final. The younger brother was not so conservative and was always on the look out for new farming equipment.

This time the younger brother was keen to buy a piece of equipment called a separator from Mr. Lloyd-Jones, who was actually the main supplier to the village of farming equipment.

As Martyn and his father turned the corner onto the farm road that led to the bachelors' farm Martyn noticed the younger bachelor running down the road. Gasping for breath he hailed the pony and trap. 'I've got to speak to you Mr. Lloyd-Jones.

I am really keen on getting that separator but I know that my brother will just disagree with everything I say. So I just wanted to explain that when you try and sell the separator to us in a few moments I will be very against it. I will be objecting to it very strongly. Just don't get confused because I really want it very much. It's just that this way my brother will think that I don't want it and so he will want it after all. Do you understand?

Now go on with you up to the farm. We'll meet you round the back. Don't say that I've been speaking to you though! Hush! Hush!'

Martyn and his father thought this was very strange but they went as agreed to the back of the farm where they met both brothers and tried to sell them the separator. The younger brother, as he had said, was very negative to the whole idea.

'We don't want one of them brother. It's just a waste of money. Its not wise at all, at all! We are opening ourselves up to financial disaster if we buy this here separator.'

'Hmph!' the older brother exclaimed. 'We'll buy it Lloyd-Jones. See we have it at the next delivery!'

Martyn and his father had a good giggle about it all the way home.

***

Llangeitho was in fact a very interesting place to live. It was amazing. The characters you found in just one little Welsh village. From champion spitter to marathon story teller, from algebra experts to unrequited lovers. They were all there in Llangeitho and Martyn had a soft spot for all of them.

But the day came when Martyn had to leave for boarding school. All that extra study had paid off. Martyn Lloyd-Jones won his scholarship to the Tregaron County School and a new chapter in his life opened up.

'Homesickness is an awful thing, as also is the feeling of loneliness, and of being destitute and unhappy which stem from it. It is difficult to define homesickness, but to me it means the consciousness of man being out of his home area and that which is dear to him. That is why it can be felt even among a host of people and amidst nature's beauty.'

Martyn Lloyd-Jones

School Days

I hate going to school!' How often have schoolboys the world over said that to their parents? Martyn felt it too. But in his case it was because he was now having to go away to school. Not the wealthy public school for rich boys that we read about, but an ordinary state school in the nearby town of Tregaron. Transport was simply too primitive in those days. Journeys by horse took far longer than trips nowadays by car, and, anyway, the Lloyd-Jones family was too poor to afford any other kind of transportation. Martyn simply had to go away.

His first impressions weren't very favourable.

'How cold this town is,' thought Martyn during his first week there. Tregaron was in fact an incredibly cold town. It was attributed to the fact that the town lies between Cors Caron (Tregaron Bog) with its dampness, and the pass of Cwm Berwyn in the mountains, which is like a funnel drawing the cold easterly winds onto the town. Everything was so different to Llangeitho. Martyn would cuddle up in his blankets and dream of home. The pretty little Welsh village nestling in the Vale of Aeron, the strong hills sheltering the little village from the cruel icy wind.

Martyn stayed in lodgings from Monday until Friday, when he was allowed to come home at the weekend.

Martyn lived for getting home. Even in the latter years of his schooling, when both his brothers had joined him, his home village of Llangeitho still had the same pull for him. Harold and Vincent would throw themselves into the school social scene. At Christmas there would be plays to put on and concerts to rehearse for. Towards the end of the term in fact lessons would cease entirely so that the pupils could put in extra effort to their shows. Martyn however didn't get involved in these things. He preferred to take advantage of the cancelled lessons to get home early for Christmas.

Both Martyn and Vincent had the extra problem of being natural left-handers. The teachers viewed this as a problem and forced both of the boys to write with their right hands. For both Martyn and Vincent this meant that for the rest of their lives they would have atrocious hand-writing.

Homesickness dogged Martyn so much that even when he was at home over the weekend he would suffer from it. He would realise that come Monday morning he would once again be travelling to Tregaron and away from Llangeitho, away from home. But to give it its due Tregaron and school wasn't all doom and gloom.

'Well Martyn, what subjects do you enjoy?' asked the kindly master Mr. Powell.

'History, sir!' Martyn would reply, eagerly. He loved learning about the past, about the great heroes of by gone times.

'And what subjects do you do best?'

'Sciences.'

It was true. For all his love of history, young Martyn shone at the sciences. But he never got over the loneliness of being away from home so young. Boarding schools, he decided, were terrible institutions. When God put you in a family, he meant you to live in it and be brought up in it, not sent away.

It wasn't just the loneliness at boarding school.

The day came when the whole Lloyd-Jones family had to leave Llangeitho and leave Wales.

'Boys,' said his father gravely one day, 'the business here in the village is finished. We can't keep the store open any more.'

This was truly upsetting news. 'I'm going to Canada to see if I can find some work.'

Canada! That was a whole ocean away. With commercial aeroplanes still a long way off (and prohibitively expensive in any case), Canada seemed far further away then than it feels now. For us Canada is just a few hours by jet. Then it could take days just to cross the Atlantic.

So Henry Lloyd-Jones crossed the ocean to seek work. Martyn's heart felt as though it would break in two on the morning that his father prepared to take his leave of them. The plan was that Mrs. Lloyd-Jones and the boys would live in part of a house near the school of Tregaron until July. By then Henry would have got settled and found a place for them. He would then send money back to buy tickets for the young family and bring them over to Canada too.

However Henry found no opportunities in Canada. He wrote back to his family often sounding totally disheartened. 'There are no opportunities for me here. This is a wonderful country for the young, and a great chance for the boys, but hopeless for a man of my age.' Tentatively Mrs. Lloyd-Jones' husband suggested that his wife start looking for other opportunities for her husband in London. His hope was that his wife might be able to arrange something through relatives and that meanwhile he could try to earn a little cash by occasional work in Winnipeg.

These were perplexing months for the whole family as Harold and Martyn were both facing crucial examinations. Mrs. Lloyd-Jones also faced increasing pressure from creditors calling out for the family to pay their debts. Mr. Lloyd-Jones eagerly awaited news of some opening in London.

In the end Mr. Lloyd-Jones announced that he was coming home and together Mrs. Lloyd-Jones and the boys went to London where they all got involved in trying to find a suitable family business for their father to run.

The whole family left Wales and arrived in London on the bank holiday weekend. There could not have been a more impressive time of the year to arrive in the capital city. They were all met at Paddington Station by Martyn's mother's brother and as they made their way back to his home Martyn's eyes became as big as saucers as he stared at his new surroundings. He was fourteen years of age and in the big city. Quite, quite different from Llangeitho. There were more shops than you could imagine and huge, great buildings everywhere. Tram cars and thousands of horses filled the streets. But tension also filled the air. The country was getting ready for war against Germany. War would be declared the following Tuesday and Europe would be in the thick of The First World War.

The Monday before war was declared Mr. Lloyd-Jones finally arrived back on British soil. Martyn went to the station to meet him. It was so good to see him once again. Together they stepped up the search to find a family business once again. None of the Lloyd-Jones' wanted to be dependant on relatives for too much longer.

But as it turned out Martyn found himself staying in London with some rather unsympathetic relatives who refused to help. These relatives ran a dairy business and resented having a pile of poverty stricken relations arriving on their doorstep. However, they would use Martyn and the other family members when it suited them and as a result Martyn had a quick crash course in running a dairy business. He would be called upon to come out in the mornings and at any time of the day or night to help run the milk rounds and make sure that everyone had their allotted quota of milk.

A milkman's job in those days was not as simple as it is today now that milk is bottled. Each of the roundsmen would either use a horse drawn cart or push a barrow round their area. The barrow would hold a large churn of milk from which the correct quantity of milk would be measured into little cans or jugs that the householders brought out.

This was all very new to Martyn but he learnt it well. Working at the dairy proved to be the most valuable lesson he had learned all year.

However, it was a traumatic time for all the family, and the separation between husband and wife and father and sons had been very painful. For a time there was the prospect that Martyn might even have to give up school to help make ends meet.

He had been willing when the family crisis arose to give up his plans to be a doctor. He would willingly have given it all up to be a bank clerk if it would have helped his family out of the difficulties that they were in and perhaps kept them together. But giving up schooling altogether was totally different and would have meant that Martyn's prospects for later life would have been quite, quite different.

But all of a sudden a dairy owner in London, fearful of what the rumbling clouds of war would do to his business, decided to sell up. It was in Marylebone, in the City of Westminster. Soon Henry Lloyd-Jones had a shop again. Young Martyn, in what we would today call his teens, found himself helping on the daily milk deliveries.

It was amazing that it was a dairy Martyn's father decided to take over. Because of what Martyn had had to do to keep his uncle sweet while lodging with him he was now familiar with the many tasks a milkman had to do. He knew all about taking the carts round the streets, measuring out the milk quotas and then tallying up the amounts at the end of the day.

Sometimes Martyn would be woken up by his father's whistle at about 5.30 a.m. when a milk man hadn't turned up to do his rounds. Martyn would then struggle out of bed to help his father with the round. Bleary eyed he would take the cart out into the dark London streets and all before doing a full day at school.

Martyn was a great help to the family business and things began to take a turn for the better. On the odd occasion Martyn's father would send an anxious plea for help to Martyn's school teacher to 'please allow my son home for the morning as we are one man down at the dairy and are in desperate need of Martyn to drive a cart.' This did not happen too often and thankfully Martyn did not have to become a full-time milkman, even though he did help at the store.

There was enough money in the family business to allow Martyn and his brothers to continue at the Marylebone Grammar School. Here his studies prospered even more than they had in Tregaron.

Martyn, aged sixteen, received confirmation one morning that his life was going to take a dramatic change for the better. A letter arrived saying that, Martyn Lloyd-Jones had been accepted as a medical student at the world famous St. Bartholomew's Hospital in London.

'The fact is that, in Western Europe at least, it was the Church which founded the Hospital... I am proud to remember that in 1923 we were celebrating the foundation of the oldest and greatest hospital in London - the Octocentenary of St. Bartholomew's. The Hospital was founded in 1123 by a Christian, a monk by the name of Rahere.'

Martyn Lloyd-Jones in an address
'Will Hospital Replace the Church?'
Christian Medical Fellowship, 1969

'I was very friendly with Martyn Lloyd-Jones... I greatly admired his intellectual approach to Medicine as a profession. I was not the only one of his friends to have these feelings and to appreciate also his humanity as a doctor.'

Sir Geoffrey L Keynes, Surgeon
on his colleague Martyn Lloyd-Jones

Martyn, the Bart's man

'You can always tell a Bart's man,' someone told the eager first year, 'but you can't tell him much!' St. Bartholomew's students at 'Bart's' as it is still known, knew they were the best! (You couldn't tell them much about medicine they didn't already know...)

St. Bartholomew's staff knew that they were working for one of the most prestigious hospitals in the world at that time. They felt that simple membership of this renowned hospital was enough to set you apart from other medical staff. They gave the impression that they were different from the rest of humanity and gave an impression of superiority. However perhaps they were allowed to think like this. St. Bartholomew's hospital was one of the very best and had an impressive showing of medical talent. Martyn Lloyd-Jones was a typical example.

St. Bartholomew's was just a short walk from St. Paul's Cathedral, one of the largest and most impressive church buildings in London. St. Bart's, as it was called, stood bang in the middle of the city of London and this was now where Martyn would spend a lot of his time getting to know the mysteries of the human body, its sicknesses and its cures.

Martyn made a lot of friends in these early years at Bart's. Many of these friendships were warm and lasting, even though apparently the opportunities to meet up were few and far between. He was popular amongst all his fellow students and very well respected for his outstanding abilities.

Martyn's commitment to medicine actually gave him an exemption from military service, unlike Harold who had chosen to study law at Aberystwyth. Harold was called up to join the Royal Welsh Fusiliers.

Such was the shortage of doctors that, as Martyn found at St. Bart's, many of the medical students who had joined the army had actually been sent back to resume their studies.

Martyn, however, wasn't totally free from the presence of war. Some years later he remembered the following instances:

'We saw many things happening for the first time ever during the War. One event was seeing the first Zeppelin to attack London. Strangely enough, instead of looking for a place to hide, we all used to run out into the street to stare at the Zeppelin and the searchlights playing on it, making it look like a huge illuminated cigar in the sky.'

'I also remember the first daylight raid by an aeroplane. The first bomb fell on a Saturday morning quite close to St. Bartholomew's Hospital... I rushed to give a helping hand.'

'Then there was one memorable Sunday night. We had gone upstairs to bed when suddenly the Northern sky became as red as a sunset for some minutes and then the colour faded out. Simultaneously there was a victorious shout to be heard with people running out into the streets rejoicing. Lieut. L Robinson had managed to shoot down the first Zeppelin above Cuffley, near Potters Bar in London.'

***

Martyn was also recognised amongst his friends and colleagues as having a very good influence over them.

'Fancy a game of cards, Martyn?' they asked him. 'All right, but no betting . . .'

'No bets? How boring!'

'Not at all - it's more fun that way. You can simply enjoy the game for its own sake that way.'

After a while his friends realized how right he was and that in fact the game was much more fun when they weren't betting and were just playing a straight game of cards

'Martyn, you're right' they would say. 'It is more fun this way!'

They did however influence Martyn in other areas and persuaded him to take up smoking, at least for a while.

***

There were other things to amuse oneself with in London besides watching bombing raids and playing cards with ones friends. Quite a few evenings would find Martyn's father waiting up until his young son wandered back home late.

'Late home again Martyn?' Henry would ask his young son. He would have a glint in his eye as he knew exactly where Martyn had been.

'Yes.' Martyn exclaimed. 'What an evening!'

'Up in the gallery again, I suppose?'

By the gallery he meant the gallery of the House of Commons which was where all the great political debates of the nation took place.

'Yes, father. I saw Winston Churchill and Lloyd-George!'

Churchill and Lloyd-George were amongst the most important politicians and orators of the time and Martyn loved nothing better than sitting in the Gallery at the House of Commons and hearing them debate with each other across the floor.

Martyn loved politics. Being near the House of Commons, he could sit in the Strangers' Gallery. This was a special place where visitors could sit and watch the public proceedings. Martyn would watch Lloyd-George the fiery Welsh orator and champion of the poor. As Prime Minister, Lloyd-George led Britain to victory in World War I. Winston Churchill was the other attraction at the Houses of Parliament. Churchill too would go on to lead Britain to victory twenty-seven years later in World War II. Martyn was present at some of the most important debates of the War. These helped him towards acquiring his own debating skills.

Martyn loved debate. His father had ensured that all his sons were familiar with the process of debating in public. They would debate amongst themselves during an evening. Sitting by the fire after tea the boys and their father would discuss issues of the day and other controversial topics. Debate was a popular pastime in the Lloyd-Jones household.

Martyn became friends with a young man called Ieuan Phillips and as a result joined Ieuan's father's Sunday school class. Ieuan Phillips also had a sister called Bethan but that's another story.

Dr. Phillip's Sunday school class had an open style. This ensured that Martyn was in his element. Martyn later recalled the excitement of Dr. Phillip's classes.

'The arguing was keen and sometimes fierce every Sunday afternoon, and very often he *(Dr. Phillips)* and I were the main speakers. I have argued a lot, and with many men during my lifetime, but I can vouch that I have never seen his like from the point of view of debate and the swiftness of his mind. He was amongst one of the best debaters I have ever met. There is nothing better for the sharpening of wits and to help a man to think clearly and orderly, than debating, and especially to debate on theological and philosophical topics.'

Sometimes debates became so excited that members from other classes (who were being disturbed) were sent to request a reduction in the noise!

It wasn't long before the old debates of the Lloyd-Jones family began in earnest once again. Before the end of the war the Lloyd-Jones family was reunited once more. Harold was invalided out of the army on account of a heart condition.

However his condition soon improved and Harold began to look forward once again to a legal career. He also took up his poetry once more and some of his verses were printed in the well-known periodical of the time, *John O' London's Weekly*. This revealed to everyone just exactly how gifted, poetically, Harold was. It was really good to have him back again.

In fact Mrs. Lloyd-Jones actually believed that Harold was the better speaker in the family but an incident occurred which perhaps casts some doubts on this. A family friend from Wales, D J Williams, was visiting the family home and had been asked to preach at a local Welsh Chapel in Holloway. Harold and Martyn went with him. They then got involved in what was quite a sticky situation. A rumour had preceded the preacher casting aspersions on his patriotism. The congregation suspected this Mr. Williams of being a pacifist. Many of the people at Holloway had sons serving on the Western Front. Mr. Williams was indeed a pacifist but was usually quite discreet about it. Unfortunately during his sermon Mr. Williams happened to make a comment which to the congregation seemed to support their suspicions.

Worshippers angrily rose to their feet to protest and condemn the preacher. Martyn nudged his brother. 'Do something Harold, they'll tear him to pieces.'

Harold froze on the spot and anxiously shook his head at his brother. He was rooted to the spot. There was no way he was going to get up there and tell these people off for heckling the preacher.

Martyn knew he had no time to lose or their friend might be dragged out of the chapel and beaten up by the furious crowd.

Striding up to the front Martyn began to address the congregation in Welsh. Silence spread across the congregation as the eloquent young man pleaded the cause of his older friend. 'I do not actually agree with the preacher in this instance,' Martyn explained, 'yet I vouch for his character - he did in fact offer himself voluntarily to the army at the outbreak of the war but was turned down on account of his poor eyesight. He is a man of integrity and honest opinion who was prepared to fight for what he believed.'

Listening to these strong words, spoken in their own language by the young, very eloquent, Martyn Lloyd-Jones, the congregation quietened down and order was soon restored.

*'The prerequisite of a path
is that it leads to a road. I
strayed, I got lost and I grew
tired on many paths...'*

Martyn Lloyd-Jones

*'The Son of God
Himself dying for us - how
can we remain so silent and
so passive? Do we spend
enough time in prayer and
silent meditation? Are we not
concentrating too much on
what we can do in public and
depending too much on our
own abilities?'*

Martyn Lloyd-Jones

Love in London

Lloyd-George, a Prime Minister of the United Kingdom had a bit too much of an eye for the girls. One girl who never returned his gaze was the beautiful Bethan, daughter of Lloyd-George's eye surgeon, Tomas Phillips. But Bethan caught Martyn's eye!

Many of us like more than one person before we meet our one true love, and get married. Martyn however was only in love with one person all his life and that person was Bethan Phillips, a very popular and vivacious young woman, and very keen on tennis.

Martyn met Bethan Phillips at the Welsh Chapel in Charing Cross Road. This was the congregation in which Martyn worshipped. It had been the congregation that the Lloyd-Jones family had worshipped in almost since arriving in London.

But though he maybe met Bethan Phillips for the first time at the Welsh Chapel in Charing Cross Road, Martyn remembered her from another place as well. It had been a summer market when Martyn had been much younger that he had first seen Bethan and she had impressed him even then.

It had been a warm summer's day and old grandfather Evans had taken his grandson with him to the market at Newcastle Emlyn. During that beautiful warm day, when Martyn whiled away the hours admiring the scenery and watching all the comings and goings, his eye had strayed to a young lass who he later learned was called Bethan Phillips.

Bethan Phillips was in fact the sister of Martyn's friend Ieuan and the daughter of Martyn's Sunday school teacher, Dr. Phillips.

Dr. Phillips as well as being a Sunday School teacher spent most of his time as an eye surgeon. He was so well-known that many important and famous people came to him for treatment, David Lloyd-George being one of his most important and well-known patients.

Bethan was quite struck with the Lloyd-Jones family when they first arrived at church. She remembered them sitting in the pew in front - a mother, a father with a large walrus moustache and three boys.

The Lloyd-Jones as regular attenders at the Welsh Chapel at Charing Cross road regularly went there every Sunday. It was the Welsh Chapel so would have seemed familiar to them - a little piece of home in the great big city that was so new. The Phillips family were already active in the church and so the affiliation between the two families began.

Like Martyn, Bethan was the middle of three children. She was the girl between two boys, Ieuan and a much younger brother, Tomas John. Bethan was a medical student too, at St. Bart's rival hospital, University College Hospital, also in London. In fact Bethan started her medical training at the University College on exactly the same day as Martyn started his at Bart's. Over the next few years there were to be periods of friendship between them. But those periods of friendship were sometimes interspersed with long gaps. It didn't matter that Martyn was best friends with Bethan's brother or that the young Martyn Lloyd-Jones was a star in her father's Sunday school class.

'He's too young,' she would complain to her older brother, Ieuan, who had got to know and like Martyn. 'He hates our pet dogs, he's hopeless at tennis and he is very serious.'

No good at all, in fact!

Bethan was mad keen on tennis. Martyn was only mediocre. He was moderately competent at playing doubles but his enthusiasm for the game in no way matched hers. In fact whenever she discussed the game in his presence he would describe it as a 'craze' which left her much annoyed.

Martyn wasn't very good at getting the young ladies on side. On one occasion he single handedly put all the feminine noses of the Literary and Debating Society meeting seriously out of joint.

He gave an address called, 'The Signs of the Times.' In this address he discussed the moral decline of the nation in many different areas. For instance he discussed the dressing habits of both males and females.

Another point in his speech was the modern bathing habits. 'The modern habit of installing a bath in each house is not only a tragedy but has been a real curse to humanity!'

Martyn went on about the rage for degrees and diplomas; newspapers and advertising; the wireless craze and wait for it - the woman of today.

He loved to bring an element of humour to all his debates and it definitely shows. Here are some of his more notorious quotes: 'If I had to spend a life-time with a companion who had one bath a day or with one who had one bath a year, I should unhesitatingly choose the latter, because a man's soul is more important that his skin.'

'There was a time when fox-hunting was the greatest sport in this country, but it has long since been replaced by divorce.'

'When I enter a house and find that they have a wireless apparatus I know at once that there is something wrong... Your five-valve sets may do wonders, they may enable you to hear the voice of America, but believe me, they will never transmit the only Voice that is worth listening to.'

'I would much prefer the young lady of the Victorian era who fainted at the sight of a mouse, to the present modern young lady who says she is afraid of nothing.'

These words brought comments from his female listeners such as: 'I hope when you are a little older you will become a little wiser!' or 'Your case is so serious that nothing but matrimony can hope to cure you!'

Thankfully Bethan did not attend this meeting or she might have totally gone off Martyn.

Unbeknownst to Martyn, however, Bethan was having second thoughts. Martyn had proposed marriage to her once and since that proposal another twenty five young gentlemen had tried their luck with Dr. Phillips' young daughter. None of them had been successful. Now, the young Miss Phillips was having second thoughts about the first proposal.

A chance meeting on the Euston Road had made her think again. She had been strolling down the street with a tennis racket under her arm when she bumped into Martyn coming in the other direction. A friendly conversation resulted and Martyn didn't make one single comment about her racket. He was in fact the perfect gentleman. There wasn't an argument in sight. But he was still a very serious young man... that hadn't changed at all.

***

Martyn was a serious young man. He had good reason to be. Tragedy had struck the Lloyd-Jones family. Harold, the handsome older brother who had returned much weakened from the horrors of the First World War, had fallen sick again. He had survived the trenches and the horrors of seeing so many friends killed, to return home and start a new life, but the young poet was also in love! However, Mrs. Lloyd-Jones was a very dominating, possessive mother, a real Evans! She forbade the love and Harold had to conduct his romance in secret.

One cold day Harold, who was still feeling a bit weak, slipped out of the house.

'Won't be long!' he called to Martyn as he shut the door. Martyn and the rest of the family took no notice and went on with whatever they were doing. Martyn was in bed sick with the flu. It was a particularly nasty bug that he had caught. One morning he had just woken up and felt really, really dizzy.

'You have the flu Martyn,' his mother said quickly tucking him back underneath the covers.

So when Harold had said goodbye and walked out the door Martyn was in no fit state to wonder if anything was up. Besides, Harold was free to do what he wanted and he was fit enough to go for a walk on his own.

However, nobody had reckoned for the explosive force of the virus that Martyn was already suffering from. Nobody reckoned that the virus that had put Martyn in bed a few hours ago would actually affect Harold in a far more serious way.

Harold walked secretly to the nearest post box with a letter for his secret love. But the cold chill that was in the air was just enough to give the flu virus the edge it needed to really run amok within Harold's system.

The winter of 1918 saw thousands of men and women who had survived a war, in which millions had been killed, die of a dreadful flu epidemic. This was long before the provision of modern medicine and things like penicillin, which nowadays we take for granted. There was not a lot that they could do for Harold.

'Will he make it?' the family asked Martyn anxiously. Mrs. Lloyd-Jones looked at Martyn who had just come down the stairs from Harold's bedroom.

Harold, weakened by war, weakened yet more by the cold on the way to post the letter, hadn't stood a chance. He had caught the dreaded flu and along with thousands of others suffered the worst effects.

Martyn stood and looked at the anxious faces of his family, the pleading eyes of his mother. They were all awaiting the awful news that he didn't want to give them.

'Will he make it?' Martyn's mother repeated.

'I'm afraid he hasn't...'

Harold didn't make it. Having survived the machine guns and the bombs of the German Army, he died, scarcely out of his teens, before the lady he loved could reach him.

Now there were just two Lloyd-Jones boys, Martyn and Vincent. Harold wasn't there any more.

There was also something else missing in Martyn's life. Something that he hadn't realized was missing before. Life did not hold the same satisfaction that it had in the past. He realized he was a sinner. He had tried too many paths and hadn't found where he was supposed to go...

*'What shadows we are
and what
shadows we pursue.'*

Martyn Lloyd-Jones

*Human endeavour at
its highest is only feeble
and ... our only hope is
that we shall be given the
Holy Spirit freely.*

Martyn Lloyd-Jones

The Medical Detective

'You'll never guess what disease Lord So and so has got!'

'A great man like that! Throwing it all away on such an immoral life.'

'I'm afraid so,' Lord Horder sighed, 'the great can be as bad as the rest of us.'

Martyn was the Chief Clinical Assistant in the Hospital to Lord Horder, the Royal Physician, the King's Doctor. Lord Horder had been called to the sickroom of Edward VII in 1910 which established him as one of the most sought-after men in private practice in Harley Street, Harley Street being one of the most famous addresses for private medicine in the United Kingdom.

How did Martyn end up as Chief Clinical Assistant to such an important doctor? It was an incident in 1920 that first brought him to the attention of Lord Horder.

The first occasion that Martyn met with Lord Horder was not that pleasant. Martyn, though he was working a full schedule at St. Bart's training to be a doctor, would still have to put in his hours at the dairy. One morning there was a particular emergency at the dairy that Martyn had to attend to. When everything was sorted Martyn took one look at the clock.

'Oh no! I'm late. Got to dash!'

He charged out of the dairy and ran frantically in the direction of St. Bartholomew's. He had an out-patients' clinic with Lord Horder and he was going to be late. Late for the top doctor in the United Kingdom. How embarrassing.

Anyway, Martyn arrived, hot and flushed and absolutely exhausted. He had already done a full day's work at the dairy and now here he was late for his out-patients' clinic. Martyn excused himself as he came in in the middle of Lord Horder's explanation of something or other and before he could gather his wits Lord Horder was firing questions at the latecomer, right left and centre.

The other students loved it of course, simply because it was someone else who was suffering under the cutting wit of the King's Physician. Martyn hesitated and dithered as the questions kept coming. Sniggers soon turned into chuckles and then eventually Martyn was the cause of gales of laughter as he got himself more and more flustered.

However, Martyn got his own back one day. That was the day that finally brought him to Lord Horder's attention in a positive light.

One day, as normal, Martyn was examining a patient. He was working as a student in an out-patient department. After some thought and the usual processes Martyn made a diagnosis of the patient. The same patient was later seen by Lord Horder when he was on a teaching round with some of his students. He took a look at the diagnosis that Martyn had proposed and was quite surprised.

'What's this then?' he said. He took a closer look at the patient. He wasn't sure if this young doctor had actually got it right. The patient's spleen was the crucial factor in the diagnosis. You had to be able to feel it before being able to make a correct diagnosis. Martyn managed it no problem. He had been able to locate the spleen on two occasions.

Lord Horder when investigating the diagnosis couldn't even locate the spleen once.

As the patient remained in hospital for further investigation it soon became apparent that Martyn's diagnosis had been the right one. Lord Horder was very interested in this young Welshman.

In 1921, when it came to the time that all the hospital appointments had to be made up, Lord Horder already knew who he wanted as his assistant. But Martyn hadn't even received the results of his examinations. This didn't matter to Lord Horder. He took the unusual step of employing Martyn even though others working alongside him highly recommended other candidates.

Martyn soon proved to everyone that he was indeed the right choice. He came away with distinctions in all his exams.

Some of the greatest in the land were Lord Horder's patients, including the infamous Lord we mentioned previously.

Martyn learned a lot from Lord Horder. 'Find out all the symptoms, even ones you hadn't considered. Not just where they ache, but what they had for breakfast, how late they went to bed, how things are going at work.' This method was first used by an ancient Greek called Socrates thousands of years ago - the Socratic method. One way of explaining this man's method of deduction is to look at how detectives on television work. You will see the detective asking a lot of questions. Some of these questions may seem to be unnecessary. But any one tiny detail can suddenly and unexpectedly give the vital clue and solve the mystery. That's what it was like being a doctor, or physician, under Lord Horder. When doctors discover what is really wrong with you, deep down, and not just the symptoms, it is called a diagnosis. Lord Horder was famous for making the correct diagnosis - he was the best in town. His eager young assistant, Martyn, soon learned the technique of being the best medical detective possible from the greatest teacher you could get.

Bethan was still as fashionable and carefree as ever - after all she did have twenty-six proposals of marriage to her name and one from one of the top young doctors in London. But Martyn was feeling rather disillusioned with life.

'All these top people with their illnesses, caused by wicked living, while the poor starve... It's the hound of heaven after me,' he explained. He felt as if it was God that was after him, making him re-evaluate his whole life and the life of the world in general.

He observed the world from his vantage point as a medical man at St. Bart's. He saw the poor and the destitute, the rich and the well-off and he saw sin in all of them. His medical training brought the young Welsh medical student into situations that would turn your blood cold. In particular when he was working in Obstetrics in some of the roughest areas of Islington he met with such a level of ungodliness that he could not have imagined when living in the delightful little village of Llangeitho. All this evil and wickedness made those days seem farther and farther away.

Martyn finally realized that, in actual fact, he was not a Christian although he had thought he was one for most of his life. He realized that it was not his chapel-going that made him a Christian, that it was not his upbringing or his pedigree that would save him. It was through Jesus' death on the cross that Martyn Lloyd-Jones could obtain forgiveness of sins.

Martyn had come to this decision through hearing a preacher at Westminster Chapel, a Dr. John Hutton. Martyn had never heard preaching like this before in his life - never at the Welsh Chapel had he heard preaching with such power. At Westminster Chapel he realized what he had been missing - a sense of spiritual reality.

If you've heard people giving their testimony of conversion, they'll often give exact times, for example 'it was Tuesday 20th October at 2.33 p.m. on a cloudy day... when I chose Jesus.' Martyn could never be so precise. To him it was a process, of God being after him, the hound of heaven following him wherever he went. For as he discovered, it isn't that we choose God, but that God chooses us.

'It was like two men walking to Tregaron,' he would explain later. 'One went on a sunny day. Suddenly it poured with rain for ten seconds. He arrived in Tregaron soaked! The other man made the same journey, and it drizzled all the way. He, too, arrived in Tregaron - soaked! They both arrived soaking wet in Tregaron. But with one man it was a sudden drenching downpour, the other solid, steady drizzle. So it is with conversion. For some it is a definite time which they remember. With others, a process, at the end of which they know that they have become a Christian. Two very different means, but the same result.'

And so it was with Martyn: the hound of heaven finally caught him. He knew he was a sinner and needed to be reconciled with God through Jesus on the Cross. Martyn had true spiritual peace at last. Joy unspeakable! The best way to hear about what Martyn thought of conversion is in his own words:

'Many listen to the gospel who have been brought up in a religious atmosphere, in religious homes, who have always gone to church and Sunday school, never missed meetings; yet they may be unsaved. They need the same salvation as the man who may have come to listen, who has never been inside a House of God before. It is the same way, the same gospel for both, and both must come in the same way. Religiosity is of no value; morality does not count; nothing matters. We are all reduced to the same level because it is "by faith", because it is "by grace."'

Martyn's life was changed beyond recognition. He had come from the position of a sinner to that of a saved sinner. Martyn who had felt as though he was spiritually blind could now see. It was a remarkable change which would affect his whole life. Soon, however his life was to change dramatically again. Martyn Lloyd-Jones would be headed in another direction. In fact his life was to change in two ways in which he could never have imagined.

***

'So you're Chief Assistant to the King's doctor, eh?' a jealous young fellow medical student observed. 'The youngest full Doctor of Medicine too - Dr. Martyn Lloyd-Jones, MD.'

Martyn had to agree, reluctantly. 'Bound effortlessly for the top too, I suppose,' his colleague added.

'Ah, you'd be wrong there...'

'What? Something to stop you on the way to wealth and fame? I can't see it.'

'Well, God can!'

God indeed had other plans for the brilliant young physician. Martyn had been sickened by all the decadence at the top. It wasn't that he had ceased to enjoy the profession of medicine. Far from it.

But in the same way in which he had longed for the home of Llangeitho while an unhappy boarder in Tregaron, he was now longing for Wales. The young man was eager to get home, home to Wales.

The 'hound of heaven', God had sent after him, had truly caught its quarry. This was not a simple nostalgia for the life of beautiful country villages Martyn had known as a child. This was a different calling: to the grimy slums and deepening poverty of industrial Wales, the smelly steel works, the drunken yobbo of the docks. Here was a dire need, a spiritual need, a people in much darkness. This was what was calling Martyn away from the bright lights of London and a successful career. He had, in his spare time, preached a few sermons at the Welsh chapel in Charing Cross Road. Now Martyn Lloyd-Jones knew that God was calling him, full-time, to preach in Wales.

Martyn was later to explain a calling to the ministry in the following way:

'A preacher is not a Christian who decides to preach, he does not just decide to do it. It is God who commands preaching, it is God who sends out preachers.'

'But my medical training hasn't been a waste of time,' he told astonished friends, as they crossed the famous courtyard at Bart's. 'You see, being a doctor has taught me how to think, how to work things out, look at what is behind the problem, not just the symptoms.'

'Just like Lord Horder taught you!'

Lord Horder though disappointed to lose such a promising young doctor as Martyn and puzzled at his choice to leave medicine was proud of Martyn too. He gave him one of his favourite science books as a recognition of Martyn's brilliant diagnoses.

'Look at South Wales today,' Martyn would exclaim. 'High unemployment, men out of work, those that have jobs are often blind drunk, fighting, abusing their families. But those are the symptoms, not the disease.'

But people still asked him 'Why give up a good profession in medicine? If you had been a bookie for instance and wanted to give that up to preach the gospel, we should understand and agree with you and say that you were doing a grand thing. But medicine - a good profession, healing the sick and relieving pain!' One man even said to him, 'If you were a solicitor and gave it up, I'd give you a pat on the back, but to give up medicine!'

'Ah well,' Martyn felt like saying, 'if you knew more about the work of a doctor you would understand. We spend most of our time getting people fit to go back to their sin!'

Martyn saw men on their sick beds and spoke to them of their immortal souls, they promised grand things, then got better and back they went to their old sin! Martyn saw he was helping them to sin and decided that he couldn't do it any more. He wanted to heal souls. 'If a man has a diseased body,' he thought 'and his soul is alright then he is alright to the end; but a man with a healthy body and a diseased soul is alright for sixty years or so and then he has to face an eternity of hell.'

To those who said he shouldn't have given up medicine Martyn would say 'We sometimes have to give up those things which are good for that which is best of all - the joy of salvation and newness of life.'

'The prerequisite of a path
is that it leads to a road. I
strayed, I got lost and I grew
tired on many paths, but I
was always aware that the
'Hound of Heaven' was
on my tracks. At last He
caught me and led me to the
"way that leads to life".'

Martyn Lloyd-Jones

*Do not give up hope
for any sinner.
Pray to God to save them.
Let not any conversion
astonish you;
be astonished rather, that
anyone should possibly
remain unconverted.'*

Martyn Lloyd-Jones

Wales' New Doctor
of the Heart

It was now the year of 1926, and the young liberal politician, Winston Churchill, was Chancellor of the Exchequer. This was the man whom Martyn had so admired in the House of Commons just before the War. Winston Churchill was a prominent politician and had taken a leading role in suppressing the General Strike earlier that year. This had enraged the Labour leader, Ramsay Macdonald, who was MP for the South Welsh seat of Aberavon. One of Ramsay Macdonald's greatest admirers in the town of Aberavon was a young Welshman called E.T. Rees. E.T. Rees was a minister used by God in the Welsh revivals. He also thought that Socialism, was the answer! 'If we get a Labour government in power, then all will be well with the world', was the way he thought. After all, wasn't the founder of the Labour Party, Keir Hardie, a Christian?

'Sad thing is,' Martyn explained to his friend Ieuan Phillips, whom God had also called to work in Wales, 'these Ministers have forgotten the Gospel, the Good News of Jesus. They've taken all the spiritual out of the Bible and turned it into just politics. Nothing wrong with politics, mind you. But it's all the symptoms again, not the disease.'

'You and your sister Bethan saw the revival twenty-one years ago,' Martyn added.

'Indeed,' Ieuan replied. 'Our father said we could always go to school again, but we might never again have the chance to witness real revival.'

So Ieuan, aged eight, and Bethan, aged six, were put on the train from London, down to South Wales, to the town of

Newcastle Emlyn, where Evan Phillips, their grandfather, had a church. There thousands had become Christians, in the 1904-05 Welsh Revival, and many who were already Christians had their spiritual lives enriched and challenged.

'But you can't live off the past,' Martyn pointed out to his friend, as they walked to the Phillips' house in Harrow. 'Memories don't save people. God does. Wales today needs to hear the real message of salvation, to repent of their sins and be born again. It's a spiritual solution they need, not politics.'

There was another reason that Martyn was going to Harrow. He would not be going to Wales alone! The beautiful Bethan, now qualified in her own right as a medical doctor, at University College Hospital in London, had continued to be a major social success. Weekend parties, tennis parties, aristocratic admirers, and twenty-five proposals of marriage since Martyn's which had been turned down.

But while many an eligible young man had crossed Bethan's path, the thought of no other woman had crossed Martyn's. Now, at last, Bethan had realized that her true friend and companion was Martyn, the younger man she had dismissed some years before. Martyn's patience was rewarded! He proposed again, and this, Bethan's twenty-seventh proposal of marriage, was finally accepted!

A journalist was waiting outside the house in Harrow. 'What a story!' he exclaimed. 'Top young London doctor, marrying highly connected Welsh beauty, gives it all up to go to the slums of Wales, to Labour leader's constituency, Aberavon. You are going to be a missionary, Dr. Lloyd-Jones? How come? This may be darkest Wales we're talking about, but hardly Africa.'

'Well, the Presbyterian Church in Wales has got mission churches in the poorer parts of Wales,' Martyn explained. 'I will be going to one of them, Bethlehem Forward Movement Church in Sandfields, Aberavon, known as 'The Forward', or simply 'Sandfields' to those who live there.'

'Isn't it a bit smelly, with the gas works, and rather rough, with all the hard men in Port Talbot docks getting drunk and violent all the time?'

'Well, the Bible says that there's hope for everyone,' Martyn replied.

'Isn't sin and salvation rather old-fashioned these days?' the journalist retorted.

'Not at all. I'm a doctor, and, as Jesus taught, it's the spiritually sick who need the cure of salvation. At least the people there know that there is something wrong in their lives.'

So Martyn and Bethan were married, in January 1927. And after the honeymoon, they moved to a grimy, terraced house in Sandfields, Aberavon. They started their married life together as a very underpaid, young minister and his wife. It was a poor church, with little money to spare.

***

'Waaah! Waaah!'

Soon Martyn and Bethan were not alone. A little girl, Elizabeth, was born in late October. A trio of dark-haired Lloyd-Jones lived happily in their new home. Word of this dynamic young preacher who had moved from London back to Wales soon spread in the town.

'Got one of the Devil's Own Generals here,' a man said nervously one Sunday. Indeed he had! Mark McCann was just that. A gaunt man, his temper and fists were notorious all round South Wales.

'What a horrible moustache!' someone would yell. Mark had an amazing moustache, of which he was inordinately proud. His fierce temper would explode if anybody ever dared insult him or his moustache! Thwack! Down on the ground would go all who dared to challenge him, felled by one vicious blow with his fist. He was a mean and able fighter, and knew it.

McCann was so violent that one day, when he came home to see his dog eating what should have been his dinner, he got out a carving knife and cut the dog's head off! Yuk! Real violence isn't like what you see in a video game. It is much nastier. McCann's violence was uncontrolled and very vicious. So one day when he appeared in church, it wasn't surprising that many people who saw him were scared stiff! Yet no one is too hard for God to convert!

That night, in 'The Forward' church in Sandfields, he met his match. He met with Jesus, who condemned his sins and then pardoned them through his death on the cross. Mark McCann, tough street fighter, repented of his sins and started his life over again, this time with Jesus as his model.

'Trouble is, Mrs. Lloyd-Jones,' Mark told Bethan, 'I can't read.'

Nor could he. From now on life was a struggle, with his violent temper and with having to learn to read long after leaving school.

'I never went to school regular,' he explained, 'I kept running away.' Bethan had to think of a book for beginners. The only one to hand was little Elizabeth's *The Red Hen*, scarcely suitable for a grown man!

'It all looks foreign to me,' muttered McCann. For McCann reading a book was like what reading Egyptian hieroglyphics would be for you and me.

'Why not try the Bible?' thought Bethan.

So they started at John's Gospel, chapter ten.

'T, H, E,' Bethan spelt out. 'That always means *the* when put together.'

Progress was slow. After a while, he seemed to be able to read bits from John's Gospel all right. But when she tried him on Mark.

'I can't read this book - even though it's got my name!'

Had McCan been memorising John 10, Bethan wondered? So they went back to John. Progress! 'I like John 14 and 15!' he said. Soon it was obvious that he needed glasses, and very proud of them he was too!

One day Martyn hardly recognised him.

'Your moustache - it's gone!'

Martyn, knowing the vicious fights McCann had got into over it in the past, was worried lest some busybody in the church had ordered him to remove it.

'Well, Doctor, I was shaving and I decided that, such things aren't for Christians! So I cut it off.'

McCann had wanted to make a clean break with his past. There was nothing wrong with having a moustache, after all. But it was the memories with it that had to go, so off it went.

One hot summer day, Bethan was asked to the McCanns' house. It was hot outside, but like a furnace inside. Mrs. McCann had the heating on full blast! Mark McCann was sitting there looking deathly pale and rigid. He was seriously ill as a result of his days spent working in the anthracite mines. In those days, many illnesses that we can cure easily today were quite incurable then. The medicines simply hadn't been discovered yet. Not even Martyn Lloyd-Jones knew a cure for this one. So Mark McCann died. But his days of savage violence, where he always had to have two friends with him before a fight, not to help him but to stop him from killing his victim after winning, were now over. He had found Jesus, the Prince of Peace, and was now in Heaven.

***

There were some other amazing converts in Aberavon. One was known as 'Staffordshire Bill'.

'Look, there's a man asleep on the fish trolley! I hope the little donkey knows how to take him home!'

'He's not asleep, I'm afraid.'

No, he was blind drunk and was being taken up the hill to his home by his faithful donkey. For the truth is that 'Staffordshire Bill' was often very drunk. It played a major role in his life. He would often be taken back in a stupor to his home, where his wife would be patiently waiting.

One night he was drinking heavily. He was in a bad way and people passed comments:

'What a stench! Don't want to be near him.'

'Foul language! Not even I swear that bad.'

'Staffordshire Bill' whose real name was William Thomas was an alcoholic and his language was awful. That night however he was sober enough to listen to what was being said by folks round about him.

'Do you know what Dr. Lloyd-Jones says?'

'No, what's he saying now?'

'There's hope for everyone!'

Hope for everyone! That meant: hope for 'Staffordshire Bill'! So one Sunday night, he was to be found outside the church. He watched them go in. But, deeply though he felt his need to enter, he just couldn't bring himself to go in.

An agonising week went by. The second Sunday came. He was once again outside the church noticing the streams of people going in to hear Dr. Lloyd-Jones. Would they really include everyone? Someone with his track record? Once again 'Staffordshire Bill' walked sadly home, unable to go in. The third Sunday came. This time he went in. There he heard that the Gospel of Jesus Christ really was for everyone!

That night he was truly converted. He may have spent many a year blind drunk, in terrible rages, but all that had now been forgiven by Jesus Christ! Staffordshire Bill was now a new man.

Some of the converts, on becoming Christians, would arrive at the Lloyd-Jones home late at night and say to a weary Martyn, 'Here's my last bottle, Doctor. I don't trust myself with it. You take it.'

Martyn, Bethan and Elizabeth never touched a drop of alcohol, especially after seeing the ruin of so many lives caused by drink. So 'Staffordshire Bill', or William, as he now preferred (the old name was too much part of his past) gave up the bottle, but he still had problems. One was with language. One day he was having problems with his socks.

He cursed out loud. This was bad news. Jesus would never want him using such profanities. So he prayed to God to help him take away such vile language from his mind, and God did. But after some while he remembered something he had said long ago about Jesus. He knocked on the door of the Lloyd-Jones house. Martyn was well used to such visits by now.

'Some years ago, Doctor,' he told Martyn, 'I called Jesus a bad name... one you wouldn't want to hear... I'm sure that's so terrible a sin he could never forgive me. I'm lost.'

'But,' Martyn explained, 'that was before you were converted. Jesus knows that. Now he is your Saviour. All your sins are forgiven!'

Martyn was able to explain that God had saved him, God had forgiven his sins - including that one - and that his salvation was secure. As many of us know, just because we become Christians doesn't mean that things will work out for us in this life. As the saying goes:

'The rain it falls upon the just
and also on the unjust fella
But mainly on the just because
The unjust's got the just's umbrella!'

Then poor William had to have a eye operation. While the surgery went well, it left him unable to read. This meant that he couldn't read the Bible any more! That really upset the man. Thankfully, Bethan's father was visiting. He was as you may remember, a famous eye surgeon in London. He took one look at William's eyes. 'It's very simple. You need extra strong glasses!'

So William got a new pair and they worked! He was able to read again. But glasses could not keep away ill health. One day Martyn was asked to visit.

'He's breathing very heavily,' Martyn observed. 'I'm afraid it's pneumonia.'

Those were the days before antibiotics. William did not recover. Thankfully he knew the Lord Jesus and went to spend eternity with him.

'The whole tragedy today is that the Christian Church is moving ponderously, slowly, heavily, while the world is in the grip of the devil. She is setting up committees to investigate the problems, and commissions to examine various situations, and calling for reports... and she is doing this while the world is on fire, and people are going to hell, and the devil is rampant everywhere.

Martyn Lloyd-Jones

Aberavon and Beyond

The medical doctors in Aberavon took a while to accept Martyn's presence in the town. To start with they were rather suspicious. After all, no one was as well qualified as he was.

But after some remarkable diagnoses, they soon overcame their fears, and realized that he was a friend, not an enemy.

Quite often if a case was really hard, they would send the patient to him, especially as he did it all for free! In those days people normally had to pay for health care. This could end up as being very expensive. But Martyn would do it for free.

On one occasion, Martyn found himself having to solve a real mystery!

There were two former St. Bartholomew's nurses who had come back down to Wales to live. One of them had a very mysterious illness. When ordinary doctors examined her, they couldn't find anything wrong. But at night, when her friend examined her, her temperature strangely shot up! Something was rather amiss... Martyn was called in to see if he could get a true diagnosis. He remembered the dragon-like ward sister for whom they had had to work. He pondered the case. Inspiration! He asked the two nurses, 'Something went wrong at Bart's, didn't it? You're not really ill at all!'

'Well, Doctor, one of us was caught - with a man in the room! It's not allowed...' The expelled nurse had pretended to be 'ill' to explain to her family back home why she had had to leave London. Her friend had come to help her.

Martyn was able to pronounce a complete cure.

***

Soon his preaching fame spread far and wide. He was asked to speak all over Wales.

One lady who looked to be at least a hundred years old asked him, 'Doctor, will you come and speak in my church every year while I'm still alive?' As the lady looked like she would soon be in the grave, he replied, 'I would be delighted!'

That old lady lived on and on! For the rest of his time in Wales, Martyn had to go every year and preach in her church.

He was even asked to go over to America to preach.

Nowadays we go to the airport and in a matter of hours we can be at the other side of the world.

But in those days, even going by aeroplane could be very slow, and it was also too expensive. So Martyn went by boat instead, and the journey took most of a week. Thus began Martyn's very happy relationship with America - when flights became cheaper and shorter, he used to fly. He spent part of many a summer preaching there.

But in those early days hardly anyone went such long distances. When they came back, it was as if they had been explorers in the jungle!

In 1937, Martyn and his young family had been in Aberavon for ten years. They were able to celebrate in a very special way! Their second daughter, Ann was born. Now they had two daughters, and Elizabeth, who had always wanted a little sister, was thrilled! 'Can I help look after little baby?' Elizabeth would ask excitedly.

Other things were happening too. So successful was Martyn as a preacher that people in other places were bound to say, 'Hmmm. That Martyn Lloyd-Jones, now he'd be a good person for our church.' Many places called Martyn, but he always said no. Then one day something happened to change all that. One of the biggest churches in London, Westminster Chapel, near where he had lived as a boy, asked Martyn if he would come and work with them. The minister, a world famous preacher called J. Campbell Morgan, was getting on in years.

'What I'd like,' he told his church, 'would be someone to co-pastor the Chapel with me for a few years, someone to whom I can hand over.'

The Chapel was huge, as big as a Cathedral. It had over 2000 people in the congregation every Sunday. For most of you a congregation that size is gigantic! Just think how many double deckers would fill a church that size!

Most people were of the opinion that 'For a church like this, we need someone truly special as the next minister. There's no doubt who that is: it must be Martyn Lloyd-Jones!'

The church that God had used in Martyn's own conversion was now calling him to work with them as co-pastor. Martyn found it difficult to know whether or not to accept. He had been ten years in Aberavon - all very special years. He had deliberately renounced fame and fortune in London to go there.

'We'll miss the friends we've made here,' he told Bethan, as they discussed it. 'But the real question is, Is God calling me to go? If he is, then it would be right to accept. But if not, then I should turn them down.' Deciding was not easy!

But in the end they had to come to the difficult decision to leave Wales, and go to London. One funny thing happened towards the end. They discovered that they still had all the alcohol bottles given to them by the converts! One night when it was pitch dark, they gave them all away to a doctor, who could use them medically in his surgery. Being teetotallers, Martyn and Bethan had not drunk a drop!

It was 1938 when Martyn, Bethan and their daughters Elizabeth and Ann went up to London. They eventually got a house in Ealing, a suburb of west London, not far away from London Airport. But what a time it was!

War was getting closer and closer! In September 1939 war began. Soon bombs were falling on London.

The little family of four, having only just moved to London, had to separate for a while, as did many families during the war, as the bombs made it too dangerous for Elizabeth and Ann. Like many children, Elizabeth and Ann had to spend some time away as evacuees. It was to be quite some while till everything got back to normal again. They had been ten years in South Wales. Little did Martyn and his family know that they would be in London, at Westminster Chapel, for thirty! The time he spent there is the next part of our story.

'M.L.-J. used to describe his understanding of guidance in this way: Think of a train standing at the departure platform. Everything is ready and waiting. Everything is checked, the engine driver has the steam up, the guard stands, green flag in hand, but the train does not move. Why not? Because they are waiting for the signal to drop! And now he was waiting for the signal to drop, waiting for that internal certainty.'

Bethan Lloyd-Jones

Westminster Chapel Days

'Wow, it's Sunday - I can't wait to go to church!' Do you feel that way on a Sunday morning? What would you feel if you were at church from 11 a.m. to 8 p.m.? Nine hours of church! Would you still be excited? For many people, Sundays at Westminster Chapel were even longer. They would travel an hour just to get there and sometimes even more.

During the wartime, 1939-1945, it could be dangerous to travel home - there might be a bomb! Once a bomb hit a building near the Chapel. BOOM! Some of the ceiling fell on Martyn's head. Thankfully he wasn't hurt, but it was quite a shock.

So people got used to staying up in town for church. After the war, people just decided to keep up the habit. And if you lived over an hour away, it would be silly to have four journeys a day two hours to and from the morning service, two hours to and from the evening service.

'Let's have Sunday School in the afternoon, after lunch but before tea,' someone suggested, and that is what they did.

The morning service had thousands of people every Sunday. Imagine over 2000 people every Sunday morning in your church! The hymns and prayers might have been like the ones you are used to on Sundays. But the sermons were different!

'The words to which I would like to call your attention this morning,' is how Martyn used to begin every Sunday morning. He found the Bible really exciting! 'It is God's word, God speaking to us!' Martyn's style of preaching was to go through the Bible very carefully, verse by verse. Sometimes, like when explaining the story of Jesus' meeting up with John the Baptist, he got so excited by what God was telling us, that he would preach on just two verses for a whole year! 'Lots of people call themselves Christians, but they have no real life in them. That's what we need: life!'

Does the study of God, called theology (Greek for God's Word) seem boring when you study it at school? 'Fire!' Martyn would proclaim, 'Theology coming through someone on fire for God! It's exciting!' Preaching he called - 'logic on fire.'

Do you remember he used to be a medical student? Examining every patient carefully and logically, working out what was really wrong with them. 'Preaching is like that: What is God saying to us? What is wrong with the world around us? That's the logic part.' God's training of him as a doctor was no coincidence. The training did not go to waste at all.

But preaching was also 'fire', God's word setting us ablaze with zeal for what he wants us to hear from and do for him. This is what made Martyn's preaching so special, why people would travel miles every Sunday just to hear him preach.

It was logical: A leads to B leads to C leads to D. But it was also on fire! It was Bible-based preaching: always on God's word, not just on Martyn's own ideas. But just as the Bible is always relevant to our needs, so too was Martyn's preaching. 'It's just as if the other 1999 people weren't here listening to him,' someone would say, 'and that his sermon was aimed directly at me!' The remarkable thing was that the other 1999 people felt exactly the same…

God's word, the Bible, however, shows how real Christians have problems all the time! Martyn knew that too, not just because the Bible taught it. He knew it because he'd get down and feel sad from time to time as well. He understood.

In his sermons, especially those for Christians on Sunday mornings, he showed how God understood too. The Bible is a supremely practical book, dealing with real life issues like no other. That is because there is no other book like the Bible! It is the only book in which God speaks directly to us. That's why Martyn always used the Bible as the basis for everything that he was preaching. He didn't just make it up, or tell lots of jokes or stories.

***

After the morning service, everyone stayed on for lunch. The Chapel had lots of rooms around the back, including two kitchens. I remember eating in the smaller eating room enjoying a baked potato for lunch. As children our baked potatoes had a criss-cross surrounded by a C for Catherwood, so that no one would eat our potatoes by mistake!

After lunch came Sunday School. Unlike many churches, Sunday School was for all ages. Bethan led the Ladies' Sunday School class, just as she had done in Wales. Bethan read her entire Bible twice a year and every Sunday afternoon for many years studied the Old Testament with the Ladies' Sunday school class. This meant that she knew the Old Testament really well. We can forget some more complicated names of Old Testament characters. Bethan would remember all of them! So when he needed reminding, Martyn would ask her. She always remembered.

There was also a mixed class for people from age sixteen until their early forties, led by Martyn's son-in-law, Fred. Many people met the person they later married at Sunday School!

After Sunday School it was time for tea! Many people sat with a different group from those with whom they had eaten lunch, so you got to know even more of the congregation than you had before.

So although many had travelled miles and miles to get to church, Westminster Chapel had a strong sense of community, of Christians being together, enjoying what the Bible calls 'fellowship'.

After tea, was the Prayer meeting, which Martyn would lead himself. People could pray for all sorts of things, and also for the needs of the church. Then there was the evening service. Martyn would preach at this one as well. Here his sermons were slightly different, in that they were aimed at non-Christians, to show them why they needed Jesus Christ as their Saviour and Lord.

'Modern people think they are so sophisticated,' Martyn would say, 'but they are in as much need of salvation as they have ever been.'

These sermons were logical and fiery too! There was the logic of the foolishness of rejecting God and the fire of the vital urgency to heed God's message. Some preachers at the end of such an evangelistic sermon make an appeal saying, 'I want you to get up and make a decision for Jesus right now!' Martyn didn't do that. He knew that if God the Holy Spirit was working in someone, that person would become a Christian without human pressure. You don't decide for God! God in his love and mercy reaches out to you, and Martyn knew this from the Bible.

But many hundreds of people were converted to Christian faith in Westminster Chapel over the years. Many would even stay behind to speak to Martyn in his study behind the pulpit after the service was over. If you preach God's word faithfully, Martyn felt, God will reap the harvest.

After the evening service, many stayed on for coffee, before going home - a final chance to chat and think about the day's events. People came not just from all over the Southeast of England. There were dozens of nationalities there as well.

'I'm from Nigeria.' 'I'm from the USA.' 'I'm from Hong Kong.'

In fact, there were few parts of the world not represented by someone at Westminster Chapel. Just like all those very different nationalities that you read about in the Day of Pentecost story in the Bible (Acts 2:1-13). There were also many students, visitors and other people from all racial groups and countries, in the Chapel every Sunday.

***

A question people ask at the weekend is 'What are you doing Friday night?' At Westminster Chapel your answer to that question might have been different to the norm. Because people came from so far and wide, it was impossible to have a midweek meeting to which everyone could come. So there was a Friday night meeting instead. People didn't have to go to work the next day, a Saturday. To begin with, it was simply a discussion group. 'So, Fred,' Martyn would begin, dealing with a particularly brave and talkative member of the audience,

'Do you really believe A, B and C?'

'Yes, Doctor, I do!' Fred exclaimed. (Everyone at the Chapel called Martyn, 'Doctor', and they usually referred to him as 'the Doctor'.)

'Well,' Martyn replied, 'that means, logically, you also must therefore believe in D, E and F as well.'

'It does?'

'Well that's if you follow your argument through properly. Now where in the Bible do you find the case for D, E and F?'

Long pause… 'Well, maybe, Doctor, D is in the Bible but not points E and F.'

'So your argument isn't fully biblically based ?'

Fred, who later married the Doctor's daughter, Elizabeth, was brave enough to try out his arguments in public, and to be a foil for Martyn to show that every argument had to be fully biblical to be true.

'Didn't Calvin say X?' someone would say.

'Yes,' the Doctor would reply, 'but on what biblical grounds did Calvin say it?'

As he said of himself, he was a 'Bible Calvinist', not a 'system Calvinist'. Calvin simply expounded the Bible, and where he did so, he was right. In other words, you have to base all you say not on what X or Y says, but on what the Bible says. After all, isn't that part of what the Reformation was all about in the first place? Instead of 'Well, the Church says', or 'St. Something wrote', or 'Pope so and so decreed', it is the Bible alone (sola scriptura) that makes Protestants Protestant. And of course, now that Martyn is no longer with us, we shouldn't say, 'Well, Dr. Lloyd-Jones used to say.' He wouldn't have wanted us to do so and it is what the Bible says, not what mere humans think about an issue that counts. As often as not, Martyn Lloyd-Jones probably never said or thought the things people attribute to him anyway. They are just using his name to give their own thoughts some authority. Martyn hated people quoting his words or anyone else's as having as much value as the Bible.

After a while, Friday evenings became so crowded that they moved to the main part of the church, and Martyn used them as occasions to go into far more depth on biblical themes. He preached on the book of Romans. He started to edit his sermons when he retired and now, over twenty years later, there is so much he was able to say that the editing process still continues!

'The struggle
is difficult, the
battle is fierce,
and we are
tempted on all
sides to back
out of it.
Hold on my
friends, fight
on, cling to the
Cross.'

Martyn
Lloyd-Jones

Feeling Down?

One great sermon series he had was on Spiritual Depression: Its Causes and Cure. People would come to see him in his little office in the church after the morning service. 'I'm feeling very sad today, Doctor,' they would sometimes say. With some he would say, 'What's your relationship with God like these days? If you're neglecting it, can you really expect to be feeling happy? Your sadness is because you're sinning.'

Sometimes it was, 'Well, we live in a spiritual battle. The Devil doesn't want you to be fulfilled in your Christian life, so he's attacking you, to make you feel bad, to reduce your spiritual effectiveness. Look at what the Bible says about resisting the Devil, about how God can help you put on the spiritual armour he's given you.'

'The Christian life isn't an easy one. It's a battle, just like the Bible says it is.'

With others, he would say, 'Actually there isn't anything spiritually wrong with you. But you need to see a good psychiatrist, because what you've got is a form of mental illness. Illness is the result of sin coming into the world. But you're down now not because of sins you've committed yourself, but rather because we live in a fallen world.'

Then with some he'd simply ask, 'When did you last have a good holiday? You're not spiritually depressed. Take a break, catch up on some sleep, and you'll be fine in no time!'

He would ask questions: 'How did you come to feel this way? How is your prayer life? Are you keeping God's rules for our lives? Are you wanting to grow spiritually? Have you been having strange dreams? Have you been working too hard?'

We're all different, all complex, each with our own very special needs and personalities. He knew that, and he knew that God had created us all different one from the other as well.

Read a book like *Spiritual Depression* and you will see what I mean. (It's only a paperback and is cheaper than a video! It is less than a burger meal and more nourishing!) It is a very realistic book.

Sometimes people will give the impression either that you shouldn't have problems or that you're somehow not very spiritual if you do. This was not the way Martyn treated people. He, too, was depressed sometimes and had to search out the reasons. Was he tired? Sinning? Sad? Working too hard? Ill? I am sure that many of you have felt depressed or sad for long periods of time: more than just for an afternoon. Being a trained doctor, Martyn knew about these things. He understood people and their feelings; he didn't condemn them for feeling sad. Rather he helped them find out why they felt as they did.

Martyn would sometimes tell those who came to see him that 'It's not just a case of snapping out of it. Sometimes the reason is medical. But sometimes God allows the devil to attack us, like Job, to test us and prepare us before he does something really big with us.'

As I said, Martyn had a long period of depression. Eventually he got better, although it took a while. One of the people who helped him was a Northern Irish businessman, Stuart Catherwood. The Lloyd-Jones and Catherwood families became friends, and the result was the marriage some years later between Frederick Catherwood and Elizabeth Lloyd-Jones, my parents.

The big things that God wanted Martyn to do were: firstly, to keep going at Westminster Chapel and secondly, to work with university students.

***

Many of you who are reading this book might be thinking about university, or will have friends, or older brothers or sisters, who are thinking about going. Often University graduates end up getting important jobs that can influence a lot of people: doctors, lawyers, scientists, MPs, teachers and pastors.

A number of my friends from University are now doing important things in the church: ministers, other kinds of leadership roles, vicars, missionaries, writers, Spring Harvest and Word Alive speakers, and things like that.

Many of us grew up a lot as Christians at University, where we learned a lot of important things for the first time. Possibly, we learned these things for ourselves for the first time! How much of what you believe do you believe for yourself? How much do you believe because you've worked it out on your own?

We'll see later in this book how important this was for Martyn's own teenage grandchildren (like me, my brother and my sister). It was important, too, for Martyn and Bethan's elder daughter, Elizabeth, who, as the war finished became a student at Oxford University for three years.

'I want to study English literature,' she said.

'English?! You want to read novels? How terrible!'

Many Christians had a funny view of the arts then, but Martyn did not. Creativity was a gift from God, after all. He loved reading historical novels himself.

'Of course you can study English - reading all that great literature!' he told her. Elizabeth had some very well-known people teaching her, including C. S. Lewis, whose Narnia stories you may have read or seen on television, or J. R. R. Tolkien, whose *Hobbit* or *Lord of the Rings* you may also have read.

One teacher made her read a famous medieval poem. Elizabeth told her, 'Why should I read this? It may be famous, but I think it's disgusting!'

Elizabeth naturally asked her father what to do. His reply was, 'Remember to read it as literature! You're there to study academically, and even if you don't like all that you have to read, you are learning, through it, how to think.'

Elizabeth and some of her fellow Christian students wouldn't go to College chapel services because they didn't like the hymns.

'The sermons they preach are sometimes very strange, too,' wrote Elizabeth. This was in the days before easy access to phones and long before e-mails were invented or even thought about.

'But you should go!' he replied, to her surprise. 'It is important not to go around giving the impression that proper Christians are always negative,' he continued. 'It is better to win people positively.'

As we can see, Martyn did not always give the answers people expected!

***

Students were important, not just his own daughter. Martyn became very involved as a speaker with the International Fellowship of Evangelical Students (IFES), and was its first proper Chairman. This combined students from all over the world, who were united by their common love of Jesus.

Martyn loved IFES especially because it not only stood for all the things that he believed in, but also because it was international. When I was a teenager, I went with him to one of the IFES conferences in a beautiful old Austrian castle.

There were students present from all over the world! From more countries than I could imagine. Of all races and colours.

But just as on the Day of Pentecost, the things which united us in Jesus Christ were far more important than the things which separated us. It was just like a foretaste of Heaven!

If you want to know more about his involvement with this student movement, you can read my book, *Martyn Lloyd-Jones: A Family Portrait*, or the chapter on Martyn Lloyd-Jones in a book entitled *Five Evangelical Leaders*.

One thing Martyn was especially keen on:

'Students must learn to think!' He would teach students to do this in many ways.

'If you're a student, it is because God gave you brains! You must use them! It is a bad witness to non-Christians when students don't do their work properly.' Of course, you can only get the grades you're capable of. Not everyone was, or is, like Martyn and his daughter Elizabeth with 'A' brains. (Elizabeth had taken notice of what her father said and gained a first class in her Anglo-Saxon English.) 'We must relate our faith to our studies, and not try to separate the two,' he would tell them.

In addition, Christianity was not just a load of nice warm fuzzy feelings, it was also true and reasonable. (Martyn didn't neglect feelings, though. As we'll see, if preaching was 'logic on fire', to use his own words, there was plenty of emotion involved!)

'Christianity, you see, is a system of beliefs. It all comes together,' he would explain.

This is what Christians call doctrine: the putting together of Christian teaching into a coherent whole. One day, one of Elizabeth's university contemporaries came to tea. He saw lots of old books on Martyn's bookshelves.

'Those are the Puritans,' Martyn explained.

One of Elizabeth's other friends, Jim (J. I. Packer, whose books like *Knowing God* and *A Passion for Holiness* you should read one day), had also discovered books by Puritan authors.

'A lot of people misunderstand the Puritans,' Martyn explained. 'They were a wonderful group of Christians who lived in the sixteenth and seventeenth centuries. Many think that they were dour and boring, a bunch of kill-joys. Not at all! They loved life! They had reason to: they loved God's things and that made them enjoy life properly!'

Jim and Elizabeth, and some other friends got very excited.

'Let's meet together to study the Puritans every year,' suggested Jim.

So they did. (Read Jim's book, *Among God's Giants* - which is called *A Quest for Godliness* in the States - and find out how this changed the lives of Jim and his cohorts.) Martyn and Jim, with lots of others, met once every year until the 1970s, and the gathering still exists, under a different name.

'We must also remember,' Martyn used to remind people to whom he spoke, 'to look at things the way God does, the way the Bible describes.'

The Puritans did this, of course. They believed in experience as well as just head belief, something which we all need reminding of today. But unlike those who simply lived off their experiences, they always tested things from the Bible.

'Was it a genuine experience?' they would ask, and Martyn reflected their strong emphasis on God's Word in his own thought and teaching. Experience, feelings, emotions, joy - all these are fine if they are tested and proved to be true from God and his Word.

Indeed, Martyn had some truly extraordinary experiences of God the Holy Spirit working in his life, and in a quite wonderful way! But he was careful both not to boast of his experiences to others and also to make sure that they were authentically from God. Elizabeth was away at university and after a few years Ann would be as well. The Lloyd-Jones' were a very close-knit family.

Martyn took a very strong interest in all that his daughters did - nothing was too trivial or unimportant for him so far as they were concerned.

'The Bible says that "children should obey their parents,"' Martyn would teach. ('Amen!' I can hear your parents saying.) But that was not all… 'The Bible also says that "fathers should not provoke their children to anger, lest they be discouraged!"' Martyn would remind all parents. ('Amen!' I can hear you saying.) To Martyn it was all a question of balance.

'As the Bible puts it, wives are to obey their husbands, but a husband must love his wife as Christ loved the church!' Look what Christ did for the church: he gave his life up for her on the cross. Now that's love! (If you who want to know more about Martyn's views on this read his best-selling book, *Life in the Spirit, in Marriage, Home and Work.*)

'Christianity,' Martyn taught, 'is reasonable. God's commands to us aren't arbitrary mean or unfair - they are always reasonable!' Our own parents might blow a fuse of anger or be unfair from time to time. But God, our Heavenly Father, is never unfair or unreasonable. He knows us! His commands are not idiotic or meaningless. He gave his only son, Jesus, to die for our sins. That is how much God loves us!

'The Christian life,' Martyn taught, 'isn't just a series of arbitrary rules. It isn't a box of "Thou shalt nots," of endless prohibitions.' Many parents make endless lists of things we can't do. But what happens when we are without our parents, and are confronted with something not 'on the list'? How do we know whether to do it or not?

'Children must discover these things for themselves,' Martyn taught. We'll see an example later in this book of how Martyn's own teenage granddaughter did precisely that.

'It's a question not merely of rules, but of your relationship to God, of wanting to please God, to do what he wants.' Rules were there for a reason, given by our loving Heavenly Father, for our good. It was also a question of 'relationship': as Christians we know God and have the Holy Spirit in us.

Keeping the rules is not something we do for its own sake, but because we love God because he has first loved us through Jesus! So we don't give up the rules when we leave home! We keep them because God is with us wherever we go.

Sometimes, in those days, Christians made silly rules, for example, never going to the cinema. Christians still do this kind of thing today. Of course, there are films which as Christians we should never want to go and see. But some films are good and wholesome, and not just those with Christian characters in them like *Chariots of Fire*.

Martyn's daughter, Elizabeth, discovered this one day. An excellent film came to Oxford.

'But,' thought Elizabeth, 'don't the rules say we should never go to the cinema?'

So she sneaked in, hoping that no one would see her…Who else should she see in the cinema, equally trying to hide in a dark corner, but the President of the Christian Union!

Of course, it may be easier to say, 'Never go to the cinema,' than to say, 'Work out what film is good and what one isn't.' But as the Bible says, the key thing is why we do something. As Martyn realized about himself, 'Doing good things can lead to sin because you can do them out of a sense of pride in your good achievements.' Or, as the joke goes, 'Aren't I wonderful, I'm so humble…!'

This is why we need to think and pray and work out what God really wants us to do. Elizabeth once wondered whether or not she should be a missionary. Some parents would burst with pride, being able to tell everyone at church, 'My daughter's a missionary, you know. Yours only works at a supermarket? Well!'

That's hardly a spiritual reason for being a missionary, is it? Now Martyn was very involved with many missionary organisations, especially the famous China Inland Mission, which is now called OMF.

On the other hand he would be very sad at his elder daughter going thousands of miles away overseas, especially since, as travel was much slower in those days before jet aircraft, it would probably mean not seeing her for years at a time!

What a dilemma! But he decided to give Elizabeth the same advice as he would give anyone in that situation.

'Does God really want you to go?' he asked her. 'Don't go round asking endless people if you're called. It might only confuse you! Take time and test whether your calling is from God.' Christian Unions can be very pressured places, where those who want to go overseas somehow look more spiritual than those who want to be solicitors, engineers or bus conductors. God equally calls people to all sorts of tasks. However, Christians tend to treat some jobs as more important than others. God doesn't.

In the end, Elizabeth didn't go, and became a schoolteacher instead. She was glad she had listened to God and what was his best for her, rather than to the opinions of those who held one job to be more valuable to God than another.

A preacher is not a Christian who decides to preach, he does not just decide to do it. It is God who commands preaching, it is God who sends out preachers.'

Martyn Lloyd-Jones

The business of preaching is not to entertain but to lead people to salvation, to teach them how to find God.'

Martyn Lloyd-Jones

A New Calling

In 1968 Martyn became very ill. He had been at Westminster Chapel for 30 years, which may be twice as long as some of you have lived. But instead of despairing, he felt that the cancer was God telling him to retire from Westminster Chapel and move on to a much wider ministry. Sometimes, when sad things happen to us, we think,

'How mean! How unfair! Why should this happen to me?'

Instead, like Martyn, we should think,

'Hmmm. What is God telling me here? Maybe he is wanting me to do something else...'

While 2000 people may seem a lot to us, there are millions worldwide who needed the kind of Christian message that Martyn Lloyd-Jones had preached Sunday by Sunday over those 30 years. So as soon as Martyn was better he began to preach in lots of struggling little churches which needed encouraging. As well as this Martyn decided to adapt his sermons into books which people all over the world could read. He sat in an old green chair and got out a battered old brown briefcase, upon which he would put the sermon transcripts. He would then edit them himself before passing them on to the publisher. But he did not work all the time...

'Croquet time!'

He and I, his eldest grandson, would team up together against Bethan and their daughter, my mother, Elizabeth. Bethan was especially good at croquet, and the women usually won 8-6 or 10-4. A good game of croquet was a nice way to relax and gave him plenty of exercise.

Sometimes he would also sleep in the old chair before getting back to work. He was in his seventies by now. The last sermons that he edited in his lifetime, but which he did not live to see finished and in print, were turned into a book called *Joy Unspeakable*. I helped see them published and got letters from people all over the world to say how much they enjoyed reading them. He could never have visited all those countries himself, or met with the millions of people who read them. Many of the books have been translated into other languages such as German, Dutch, Spanish and Korean. Nearly twenty years after his death, I met a young Korean who had read Martyn's sermons in his own language!

***

'Dacu!' I would call out when I saw Martyn.

'Dacu,' pronounced Dah-kee, was the name I invented for my grandfather when I was small. Martyn was my mother's father and she gave me his name: Christopher Martyn Stuart Catherwood. Many people held Martyn, the Doctor, in great awe. Often they were silent in his presence, too nervous to speak. Martyn himself was and remained rather shy.

'Hello, Mr. Smith,' he would say to someone, and even if he had known someone for over forty years, he would still say, for example, 'Mr. Stott,' or 'Dr. Packer' rather than 'John' or 'Jim'. Ever since the 1940s, several hundred church ministers (maybe yours included, if he is old enough) would gather together regularly in Westminster Chapel to discuss points of common concern, interest, or anxiety.

'Doctor! Some of the teenagers in my church have come with green hair!'

'Well, Mr. Smith, how are they doing spiritually?'

'Well, Doctor, they're bringing along their unconverted friends, and taking part in the prayer meeting regularly.'

'So, spiritually they are progressing well?'

As with the Friday night meetings and in the chats he had in his little study, the Doctor helped people to think both biblically and for themselves. If you work something out for yourself, you are more likely to remember it than if you are spoon-fed. You ended up, thanks to his questions, by answering the matter yourself. He probably knew the answer, but rather than simply telling you, he enabled you to think it through and come up with the answer yourself. This is what he did with all those ministers, for over thirty years. They would also telephone him as well. Sometimes Martyn and I would be in the middle of a conversation...

'So, Christopher, how's it going with your A levels?' he would be asking me.

'Well in history we learned all about Lloyd-George.'

'Ah! Now I remember him making that speech - I was in the Gallery of the House of Commons at the time, exactly the same age that you are now. He said...'

Brrrring! Brrrring! A phone call.

'Doctor! All the teenagers in my church have started listening to rock music...' an anxious voice would say on the other end of the line.

A long conversation would then follow, during which I would join my grandmother in the kitchen.

After a while...

'Ah Christopher, about Lloyd-George...'

For several months of the year, Martyn and Bethan would stay in our Cambridgeshire home. There he could write, work and think without the telephone! Having been a medical doctor and then a preacher in one of the roughest and poorest parts of South Wales, nothing shocked him much! Rather, sin and the reason for sin saddened and appalled him greatly. But we were all born sinners, as the Bible tells us 'none of us is righteous'. That is why, of course, only Jesus could be our saviour. As a result, people could and did talk to him about anything. This was especially true of teenagers, many of whom did not, unlike their parents, know he was famous! Often the teenager would find him all friendly and relaxing, when the parents were too nervous to speak! One reason is that he always took people and their concerns at their own valuation, not other people's.

'Dacu! The boy doesn't fancy me...'

Rather than dismiss his granddaughter's anguish as mere teenage moping, he would give great sympathy and advice.

***

Martyn and Bethan Lloyd-Jones had six grandchildren altogether. The three children of Elizabeth are: Christopher Martyn, the eldest (myself), Bethan (named after her grandmother) and Jonathan. The three children of Ann are: Elizabeth (named after her aunt), Rhiannon and Adam Martyn.

Let me give several illustrations of Martyn Lloyd-Jones as the grandfather of teenage or near teenage grandchildren.

In my own case, one reason for my closeness to my grandfather was a shared love of history. I can see the history books that he gave to me even as I write this. I still enjoy reading them many years later. I must confess that I was never a wild rebel as a teenager. (Note: Secretly, many of you aren't wild either! If you are one of those who secretly does homework in the middle of the night when no one is looking, and scrubs out your name from the top of the lists at school so that no one will discover you have lots of brains, read on...) But even if we're well-behaved, that doesn't make us Christians! Being immensely good, helping old ladies cross the street, making all the beds for your mother, none of that makes you a Christian. The Bible says that everyone is born a sinner, in a state of fundamental rebellion against God.

Another thing that doesn't make you a Christian is having Christian parents. You can't inherit Christian faith like you inherit dark hair, or blue eyes, or a tendency to freckles. I had two Christian parents, four Christian grandparents. With my mother's mother's family (Bethan and the Phillips), I had Christian ancestors stretching way back into the eighteenth century. That is a lot of Christian ancestors! Yet not a single one of them made the slightest difference as to whether I was a Christian or not. For as Jesus told Nicodemus, 'You must be born again!'

One day my grandfather was preaching in a service in Westminster Chapel. 'You may be deeply involved with church,' he was explaining, 'but not a Christian.' Or as Billy Graham put it a few years later,

'You may even be a deacon in your church, but you still need to be born again!'

'Hmmm. . . ,' I thought. A long process began, at the end of which I knew I had become a Christian. God has no grandchildren - only children. But God used a sermon of my grandfather's to begin a process that led me to my own faith in Jesus Christ. Maybe you need to think about whether your faith is truly your own, or just a reflection of your family's. Certainly, Martyn and Bethan never pressurised their family into 'making decisions'. You can't anyway! True Christian birth has to come from within, not family pressure from outside. You can't lead your child to Christ: Christ leads us to himself.

Rebels? OK - you can start reading again now! This bit applies to you! Dr. Lloyd-Jones never used personal family illustrations from the pulpit. Quite apart from anything else, it was unfair on the family! But these illustrations are given with the permission of my brother and sister - so it's all right to include them... (just in case you were wondering). My sister, Bethan, was a big fan of Manchester United, and especially of their star player George Best. I am sure your parents will remember him well. She took a magazine called FAB 208 (after a radio station) in which he had a ghost-written column. She heard one day that he was going to make a special appearance near home. Excitement! Unfortunately for Bethan, the day of the visit was a Sunday.

'You can't go,' said our father, 'and that's final!'

'BUT I WANT TO GO!'

'No: You AREN'T GOING!'

In the end, my parents asked our Dacu (as we all called our grandfather), in the hope that his authority would tip the scales.

'But of course she should go!'

'Don't you mean shouldn't go?'

'No - should go! What is she going to think of Church if it is some boring place to which she is forced to go against her will? God must work directly with her, convicting her of what is right and wrong.'

So Bethan (and my mother) went. The day was cold and very foggy. Lots of teenage girls stood shivering and waiting and waiting and waiting ...

'Where's George Best?' they wailed. Where indeed? In fact, he never turned up. How much better if Bethan had been all warm, inside and at Sunday School with her friends... But, as her grandfather had predicted, this discovery Bethan had made for herself. It wasn't long before Bethan too became a Christian, in the kind of big tent evangelistic event, with choirs, altar calls and everything of the kind that Martyn disapproved. (Westminster Chapel had no choir - just the voices of 2000 people singing!) But not only did Bethan go forward at an altar call, she was actually one of the singers in the choir! Did her grandfather mind? Did he say, 'Well, she's not been converted through good, sound "Reformed teaching"'?

'Not at all!' as he would say. His eldest granddaughter had been truly converted! Hallelujah!

***

Similarly, when I was a student at university, and learning a lot of deep spiritual truths all over again for myself, I went to a Church of England. Now, in the last fifteen years of his life, my grandfather had some big reservations about many things in the Anglican Church. But his question was, 'Will Christopher grow spiritually there? Will it help him?' rather than, 'An Anglican church! How dare you!'

He came to Oxford to preach in my final year. There was a wonderful Welsh President of the Christian Union, Lindsay Brown, a historian in my year. 'Your grandfather was rather good,' said a surprised young Anglican student. 'I never knew Martyn Lloyd-Jones was still alive. I thought he was one of those great nineteenth-century preachers like Spurgeon!'

***

With Jonathan, it was rebellion on a slightly greater scale than going to see George Best on Sunday or attending an Anglican Church.

My brother was into rock music (very loud), unusual cigarettes and, for a while, dropping out of school and playing briefly in a rock group. (How is that for 'street cred'?) Jonathan was also into Tibetan mysticism in a big way, as now are many other people since film stars such as Richard Gere and films like *Seven Years in Tibet* and *Kundun* have made it very popular. My brother, though, was ahead of the trend: like his grandmother Bethan (when she was a teenager), he set fashion rather than follow slavishly what other people did. Rather than come down heavy-handed, my grandfather decided to befriend his middle grandson, and find out what was important to him. Although the deacons at Westminster Chapel were always getting on Jonathan's case, expecting him to behave better than any other boy his age because well, 'He is the Doctor's grandson you know...'

However, Dacu knew and recognised Jonathan as an individual. He would say 'Well not only has God no grandchildren, but Jonathan is his own person, not simply my grandson!' Both Jonathan and his grandfather loved to play billiards (we had our own table) and the Doctor and Jonathan would play for hours on end, Dacu listening carefully to him, discovering patiently about his view of life. Teenagers were people too!

'My favourite book is *The Third Eye*,' Jonathan explained one day, handing his grandfather a lurid covered book with a greenish face on the dust jacket, complete with a third eye on the forehead. 'Tibetans understand the Universe as it really is,' he continued, as our Dacu waited patiently and potted another ball into the corner pocket.

Rather than throwing the book into the bin with some remark like, 'How dare you read such filth!', Dacu accepted it graciously and took it home with him. Soon afterwards, he was speaking to thousands of Christians, at a big meeting in the north of England. He went by train, and on the way back took out the book given him by Jonathan. He hoped that no one who had heard him preach that night would see him reading a book with such a strange cover!

But the subject matter was important to his grandson, and so it was important to him, too. Not only did he read it, but he took careful notes, so that he could chat about it knowledgeably and in proper detail with Jonathan. He also did some detective work. The real author of the book wasn't a Tibetan monk, but someone from London who had written about experiences that he had never had himself, let alone in Tibet!

'Imagine that, Jonathan, this man was writing about mystical insights not in a Tibetan monastery, but probably invented not far from us here in London.' Once again, Martyn Lloyd-Jones did not dismiss out of hand the symptoms. 'Huh! Teenagers! Long hair! Men with earrings!' Rather he looked within.

'If someone is reading about Tibetan mysticism, he must be seeking something deeper. Yes, so much of twentieth-century materialism is shallow. Yes, there is a spiritual reality behind the outward material world which we see. Yes, we do have souls as well as bodies. Anyone asking these kinds of questions about life is seeking the truth. But the answer isn't the Dalai Lama. The answer is Jesus Christ, crucified and risen!'

Thankfully Jonathan no longer believes in mysticism, and has rejected completely all artificial ways of escape from the realities of life. He didn't change overnight. He made it not by being yelled at, but by himself, working out his own relationship with God. Both Jonathan and I have had many big ups and downs in life since we lost our Dacu in 1981. He died, in fact, on my 26th birthday. But the Bible is a very realistic book! It never promises Christians a bed of roses. In fact Jonathan and I got to know Christians in countries where professing faith in Jesus could land you in jail! We should thank God for the freedom he has given to us - a freedom that many Christians today do not have.

***

In some families, everyone reads a newspaper or sits around a blaring television at mealtime. This was never the case when Martyn and Bethan came to the Cambridgeshire home of Elizabeth and her family. Our grandfather loved discussion. He particularly enjoyed it with his teenage grandchildren. Our father revered 'the Doctor' and was in awe of his illustrious father-in-law. To us, however, although we knew he was world famous, we never thought about it when he was with us. We loved him deeply. He was our grandfather. He was simply the most wonderful grandfather ever! The main thing about him was that he was approachable, so we could relax in his presence.

He, in turn, liked a good discussion, and since all too many people were overawed by him, he knew that with us there would be people who would answer back! This astonished our parents, but he didn't mind! One important thing: 'Don't feel you have to say something or believe something just because I do,' he would always tell us. He didn't want either boring conformists, or little diplomats who would tell him one thing but privately believe another. Sometimes he would just stir it up, to see what happened.

'I believe X,' and he made some outrageous statement.

'Dacu - you can't!'

'All right then - why not?'

Pause.

'Well, I think A, B and C.'

'Yes, but C is nonsense, so A and B are shaky.' 'Hmmm. But A and B are right because D, E and F?' 'Ah! So why do you believe D, E and, above all, F?'

Pause.

'Well, surely G and H!'

Actually, he too believed A, B, C and D and probably E and F as well. But he wasn't going to tell us! He wanted to know why we believed them. He loved to see what we read. We were given lots of books at Christmas, and he used to look at each of the volumes we had chosen and ask,

'Why have you chosen this one? Does it interest you? What made you become excited in this subject?' Sometimes he would be reading book reviews in one of his favourite newspapers. He read slowly, so often read the Sunday papers during the week. One particular book review would catch his eye.

'Aha!' he would twinkle. The phone would go in our home. 'This is Dacu speaking. Do you have Lady Jane Grey's biography? You don't? Then I will buy it for you.'

Sometimes he would choose a gift for a special occasion. He also bought me a new Bible for my own personal reading when away at university. The biography of Lady Jane Grey, is a book that I still have and keep now on the bookshelves I inherited from him. Christmases since he died, now nearly twenty years ago, have never quite been the same. But he gave us a love of books and a desire to find out what people are thinking and what interests them.

***

Christians are not immune from sorrow, unemployment, illness or personal tragedy. Martyn's three youngest grandchildren, Elizabeth, Rhiannon and Adam, saw their father leave their mother, before the two younger ones had even turned ten. (Happily their mother found a wonderful new husband, but not straight away.) Being the children and grandchildren of Martyn Lloyd-Jones was no protection from the sad fate of marital break-up. You may know some friends at school and maybe even people in your own family who have gone through a separation or divorce. But their Dacu was there for them, doing all he could to support them, knowing that ultimately his daughter Ann and her three little children were all in God's hands. His brother, Vincent, our beloved great-uncle, died a recovered alcoholic. A warm, loving, kindly, gentle great-uncle, the stresses and strains of his job were just too much. Like their grandfather, 'Old Evans', drink became too close a friend. But the two brothers remained close always, even if Uncle Vincent's hand would shake so much that he spilt his hot tea everywhere whenever he came over to visit. The two brothers loved puns.

'Bet you can't make a sudden pun on any word...'

'Of course I can!'

'All right - how about Japanese?'

'Oh, give a Japanese one ...' (= a chap an easy one). Vincent and Martyn had been brought up by the same parents, gone to the same church when young and both enjoyed a similar sense of humour. In worldly terms Uncle Vincent had done very well. He was Sir Vincent, with a big house in central London. His lodger was a Lord! He had regular invitations from the Queen to Buckingham Palace. But what a sad way to end so distinguished a career... What good was worldly success, a title, money, famous friends? Martyn had given all this up in 1926, to go to the slums of Wales. He never had much money in life. But who was happier? When Martyn, towards the end of his life, was offered an honour, he said no.

Martyn said emphatically, 'I am a Doctor of Medicine of London University, and that is enough!' On his tombstone in Wales, he went one further and put a quote from the Bible, 'For I determined not to know anything among you, save Jesus Christ, and him crucified.' These were the words of the Apostle Paul in writing to the church at Corinth (I Cor. 2: 2). Rather fittingly these were also the words Martyn had used as his text in 1977, when he returned to Sandfields in Aberavon for the 50th Anniversary service of his arrival there as a young preacher in 1927.

He was buried in Gelli cemetery in South Wales, in the graveyard of his wife's family, the Phillipses. His own family, the Jones and the Evans had, in the past, never been particularly Christian and he wanted to be associated with his godly, Christ-minded in-laws. Almost exactly ten years later, his beloved Bethan was buried next to him. By that time, their first great-grandchild, Myfanwy was born, just old enough to attend the funeral. There are now four great-grandchildren: Myfanwy, Angharad, Jamie and Elizabeth. What a life was Martyn's! A life dedicated to the service of God, to proclaiming the Good News of Jesus, just as proclaimed on his tombstone. A life, too, against the odds. As we saw at the beginning he did not exactly have an easy start in life, with a drunken grandfather, a financially hard-up father, a difficult time of separation from his family. But God was in control and guided Martyn throughout his life. Think for a minute. Is God your guide?

Your twenties might seem ancient to you, but it isn't really. In Martyn's twenties he had massive success as a student and a doctor, only for it to be given up to go back to poverty in Wales! Martyn surrendered his life to God's plans and he ended up by becoming world famous.

My wife Paulette teaches piano. A sweet little Japanese girl came one day as a pupil, along with her mother. Mrs. Sugino saw a picture of Dr. Lloyd-Jones on our wall, and loads of copies of his books.

'Dr. Lloyd-Jones! Why I have read him - in Japanese!'

We had never met this woman before. She and her family were only in Britain for a short while. They were therefore hardly family friends! Yet every music lesson, while her daughter played the piano, Mrs. Sugino would sit in the room (near or in the chair where the books were written) and read the English versions of many of his books. Nearly twenty years after his death those books have sold millions of copies, as we have seen. Martyn gave up fame and fortune in 1927. He certainly never gained a fortune. But fame he had a plenty!

Martyn would surely in time have become the Royal doctor, just like his old boss, Lord Horder. He might have ended up being called Lord Lloyd-Jones of Llangeitho.

Have you heard of Sir Ronald Bodley Scott or Lord Evans? I rather doubt it! But you probably have heard of Martyn Lloyd-Jones, or you wouldn't be reading this book! Through his own ministry, and that of his books (such as *Spiritual Depression*, still in print for probably longer than your parents have been alive), Martyn Lloyd-Jones was able to help millions of people, most of whom, like my wife Paulette, never met him when he was alive. He did something far more important than being a top doctor or earning heaps of money. He helped to point people to Jesus Christ, the doctor and healer of our souls. You can't do more than that!

*The gospel tells us
that our most sacred
thoughts, our deepest
affections, our sublimest
emotions are as nothing
compared with what we
shall experience when
we meet our
Saviour
face to face...*

Martyn Lloyd-Jones

Heaven:
The Christian's Real Home

Have you ever known someone who has died? A grandparent, perhaps, or some elderly lady down the street? Perhaps somebody you know has died unexpectedly young? I think that it is time to say that when you attend the funeral, it makes all the difference whether or not the person who died was a Christian. Death is far from being the end - in fact it is only the beginning of eternal life with God in heaven. When Martyn preached at funerals, as a minister, it made a huge difference to how he preached, on whether the person who died, and those who knew him or her, were Christian. When his own father died, back in the 1920s, Martyn was understandably very upset. An American friend, Carl Henry, some fifty years later said to him, 'Tell me, Doctor, was your father a Christian?'

Martyn looked very sad, and a tear came into his eye.

'I don't know,' he replied. But when his friend David died, around the same time that Carl Henry asked his question, it was very different.

'David died young,' Martyn told his widow, Shirley and the assembled family, 'after a long and terrible illness, made worse by all the mistakes the hospital made.'

As we've seen, Christians aren't exempt from things going wrong, and in David's case, they went seriously wrong, so that he was stuck in bed for months, unable to speak or move.

'Now David has left behind a widow and five children, some still in their teens,' the Doctor continued. 'But David was a true Christian. A local doctor - we were both medical men - all his patients knew of his clear Christian faith and witness. People in the town thought so highly of him that they asked him to be their Mayor!' So popular had David been, in fact, that the church was filled with local townspeople as well as friends and family.

'Now, after all this suffering, he is with Jesus in Heaven!' Martyn proclaimed.

'The family aren't going to sue the hospital for their mistakes. It won't bring David back to life, and since he's now in Heaven with Jesus he is in the best place of all!' Martyn explained what it was that David believed, about having Jesus as your saviour and Lord.

'Christianity is not a message of despair, but one of hope! Jesus died on the cross, for our sins. But on the third day, he rose from the dead! He is now with his Father in Heaven, where David has joined him. Jesus conquered sin and death! Death has no fear for Christians any more, not after what Jesus did!'

'David's family will miss him terribly. We all will. But death is not the end, not for Christians. For Christians, death is sad. But death is a reminder of the victory of Jesus. A funeral can be a time of thanksgiving for a life that was faithful, like David's was, and a reminder of things to come.'

Martyn's funeral speech made a big impact. Not only was a member of David's own family converted, but so were other members of the congregation who had come in from the town. A physical death led to spiritual new life for many! As we've seen, in 1968, aged sixty-eight, Martyn became very ill with cancer. But instead of complaining about his fate, he asked himself, 'What does God mean me to do now? What is he using this illness to tell me?'

Firstly, as the surgery was completely successful, in itself remarkable for a man of 68 with so serious a dose of cancer,

Martyn knew that life was now a kind of 'extra time' from God. He was fortunate to be alive! I deliberately haven't said lucky, because, as Christians, we surely don't believe in luck? How does a random concept like luck tie in with what we know for sure of God's love and provision for our lives?

So for the next twelve years, Martyn preached all over Britain, spoke and taught in America, and, to our tremendous joy, spent even more time with us in our house in Cambridgeshire, turning his sermons into books. Then in 1980, he fell seriously ill again with cancer: not a relapse from his 1968 illness, but a completely new and gravely complex growth. I spent some of 1980 far away in China.

'How long will Christopher be away for?' he asked. My time in China was busy, but occasionally I would stop and think, 'I wonder how Dacu is? Will I see him again?' Much of the Chinese countryside was very remote, and it was not possible for my family to get hold of me in a village in the middle of nowhere.

Thankfully Dacu was alive when I returned, but he was now extremely thin and gaunt. Being a doctor, though, he was fascinated by his own treatment. His grandson, my brother Jonathan, would hold him by the arm and take him for painfully slow walks around the garden. He had to give up croquet though as he was now too ill to play.

December 1980 saw me in Luxembourg and France. I came home on the train with one of my cousins who was studying in France.

Poor Martyn was now too ill even to read books! I bought him the Christmas edition of, *The Illustrated London News*, which was solid enough for him to enjoy for his eighty-first birthday, but not too long so as to make him overtired.

By early 1981, he had lost his voice. This meant that he had to write everything and as you will remember, because he and his brother Vincent were natural left-handers and forced to write with their right hands all those many years ago, their handwriting was terrible! (Through no fault of their own, of course.) So he would write us little notes, as his only way of communicating with us.

March 1st approached - my birthday. I was to be twenty-six. I had plans to go off to see Christian friends in Austria, Denmark and also the old Yugoslavia. But as Martyn was seriously ill, I had to consider, 'Should I go?' It being the weekend of my birthday, Elizabeth and her family, including myself, were all in Cambridgeshire. We had a friend, Jane, staying with us. As she was medical as well, she spent the weekend making alphabet cards to help my grandfather to communicate. He might soon be too weak even to write. Normally people pray hard for healing when a loved one is ill! Not Martyn.

'Don't pray for healing,' he told his family, 'Don't try to hold me back from the Glory.'

From 'the Glory'? Yes, from Heaven. He knew that his entry to Heaven was now coming. So much so in fact that he cancelled his newspapers to stop on Saturday, February 28th. Martyn had loved reading the news all his life.

That night, he and Bethan went to bed. He remembered that my birthday was the next day and made a note of this to show Bethan. He never woke up. He died early in the morning of Sunday March 1st. He had been right - he wouldn't need any more newspapers! It was very appropriate that he died on God's day, Sunday, the day we not only go to church, but celebrate the resurrection of Jesus. Martyn Lloyd-Jones' body was dead - it was rather creepy to see it there, just after we had rushed up to London to be with and comfort Bethan, his widow. But Martyn's soul was alive! In Heaven with Jesus!

March 1st is also St. David's Day, the national day of Wales. Few were more patriotic than Martyn, and there too the symbolism was perfect. The little town of Newcastle Emlyn was jam-packed for his funeral. He had, in fact, made all the arrangements himself not long before, so we knew what to do. It was a sad occasion, because we all missed him, and everyone who knew him in life, his family especially, still does miss him a lot. But it was a triumphal thanksgiving to God, to thank him for the huge privilege God had given us for the unique and wonderful life of Martyn Lloyd-Jones. What a life it had been! And as he would have wanted us to say, what a great God!

The following additional chapters give a deeper understanding of the life of Martyn Lloyd-Jones.

Pages 141 to 152 are a selection of Thinking Further Topics which will help you to think through the life of Martyn Lloyd-Jones for yourself. These should also help you to think about your own life and what you can learn from the life of Dr. Martyn Lloyd-Jones.

Unspeakable Joy

It was a very hot, wet day in Tsimshatsui. Monsoon rains were pouring down heavily. When it rained in that part of the world, it rained. Humidity was 100% and walking anywhere was like strolling through a steam bath. It was the end of the rainy season and I was glad that I would soon be in the drier climate of northern China. The lack of pollution controls with all the industrial stench wafting everywhere unchecked, plus the pungent aroma of spicy cooking coming out of the windows, all combined together to produce one very unforgettable and overwhelming smell!

I was seeing an Australian missionary who had lived for a long time in Borneo. I asked him some questions about my forthcoming trip to Peking. Then he turned to me and asked me out of the blue,

'Tell me, was your grandfather a Pentecostal?'

Martyn Lloyd-Jones a Pentecostal? And how had an Australian living in Borneo heard of such a thing?

Some years later, I was on the other side of the Pacific in an American megachurch in California. A burly man, muscular and tall, came up to me, with an almost menacing air.

'They tell me that some people fixed the Doctor's sermons to make them look Pentecostal.'

'Actually, that's not true,' said a friend of mine, coming to the rescue. 'I read the book, and I listened to the tapes of the Doctor's sermons. It's not true.'

Martyn Lloyd-Jones the Pentecostal? Martyn Lloyd-Jones the anti-charismatic, the victim of a dastardly Pentecostal plot?

Great men always have followers who want to claim them exclusively for themselves. These followers of Martyn Lloyd-Jones wanted to appropriate him for their own views, to say that he was really on their side, and because he was right, they must be too! This is particularly true of the issue of 'gifts of the Spirit'. Pentecostals and charismatics seem to take one side and those who take the traditional view the other.

Historically, those who take the 'Reformed' view, the followers of the great sixteenth-century French Reformer Calvin, argue that the miraculous gifts from God that we see in accounts such as the book of Acts, or in biblical letters such as Corinthians have long since ceased. This is called the 'cessationist' view.

Those who are called charismatics or Pentecostals say that this view of the Bible is wrong, and that all these miraculous gifts, such as healing and prophecy, still exist for Christians today.

Many Pentecostals, in particular, say that the 'gift of tongues', or speaking in an unknown language, is the required proof of a special blessing from God that the Bible refers to as the 'baptism with the Holy Spirit.'

Just to confuse us all further, there are many who say that you can be a 'Reformed charismatic', two historically contrasting doctrines, all at the same time!

Bethan always disliked all the labels that people give themselves. She used to say 'Why can't people just be biblical?' But as we used to point out to her, all these people said that they were biblical! (Not their opponents of course...)

So why is all this important for an understanding of Martyn's life? Firstly, you may have heard one set of things about what he believed and taught, and then met other young people from another church who firmly believe that he taught the exact opposite? They aren't trying to mislead you - they really believe it! Secondly, what I want to do is to take this as an issue, and get you to do what he would have wished for you to do: namely, go back to the Bible and work it our for yourself.

Remember that on Friday nights, Martyn would always ask the people at Westminster Chapel to base their arguments on the Bible.

'Surely, Doctor, Calvin said...'

'Ah, but what does the Apostle Paul say?' Martyn would retort.

As we saw, Martyn always referred to himself as a Bible Calvinist, not a system Calvinist. Calvin was right about so many crucial doctrines because he simply expounded the clear teaching of Scripture. But that doesn't mean that Calvin was always right, does it? As we know from history, even the great Reformers, such as Calvin and Luther disagreed with each other on many things.

What they all agreed upon were the core biblical teachings, such as salvation through Christ on the Cross, something upon which all true Christians agree today.

Maybe you are a Baptist, or perhaps you are a Presbyterian. If you are a Presbyterian then you'll have quite a different view of baptism, from your Baptist friends. But in all likelihood, you'll come from a church that calls itself Evangelical, whether it is Baptist or Presbyterian. So although you differ on one issue - baptism - you're united on all the things that really matter, such as Jesus and what the Bible calls the Good News of salvation. Real Christians can agree on the essentials while differing on other issues. This is because sincere Christians have come to differing conclusions often based on the same verses!

But as Martyn never hesitated to say to his teenage grandchildren around the kitchen table, the main thing is to base your conclusions on the Bible, rather than getting them second-hand from someone else. That sometimes meant that we disagreed with Martyn himself! He never minded that, though, so long as our views were Bible-based. He knew he wasn't infallible, even if many of his followers sometimes seemed to claim infallibility on his behalf!

Being a Protestant, not Catholic, Christian, he knew from the Bible that it is the Bible itself, God's word, that is without error and not humans, like us!

I once had a coffee with a close friend of Martyn's called Hywel.

'Your grandfather was concerned about life,' said Hywel. 'Look at the Bible, and all the references to life. How many churches today, even if they have all the right doctrines in their heads, have life?'

Life! Real life! Being alive! Do you know churches that seem to be dead right: theologically correct but really boring?

Then do you know churches that are full of life, growing rapidly, lots of converts, filled with the sheer joy of being born again in Jesus, but with several really weird doctrinal views because their theology is in a bit of a muddle? This kind of thing really worried Martyn. He believed passionately in correct doctrine. As we've seen, preaching to him was 'logic on fire'. Yet all too often he saw churches with all the logic of correct belief but none of the fire, and other churches on fire with their love of Jesus but none of the logic of proper doctrine based upon the Bible. Something was rather wrong!

Surely what was really wanted were churches that were both doctrinally correct and very much alive! So in the 1960s, Martyn concentrated his preaching in the mornings at Westminster Chapel on this issue: life! He based it upon the early chapters of John's Gospel. As I write this, the early sermons have already been published, and the later sermons on this theme will appear about the same time as this book. The tapes of all the sermons have been available for many years. You can hear his very words to the congregation if you are the kind of person who prefers listening to a tape instead of sitting quietly with a book.

The first published series, *Joy Unspeakable*, was edited by Martyn in his lifetime, but did not appear in print until shortly after his death. What a row it caused! I now teach in Cambridge, but at the time worked for the publisher who brought out the book, and to whom Martyn had given the sermons before he died. I had phone calls:

'Well done! How wonderful to see these sermons in print! Now people will know what he really taught.'

'How dare you! These sermons should never have been published! They will cause complete confusion.'

Oh dear. What a muddle!

Each side said that Martyn was really on their side: certainly not on the other! Much ink was spilt. Words were exchanged. It was sometimes hard to avoid the conclusion that Martyn was like a football being kicked about by opposing sides, and on quite a few occasions his family felt a bit like a football too - kicked heavily by both sides at once! It is also impossible to avoid the feeling that Martyn himself would have been deeply saddened. This is because people were arguing about what Martyn taught, whether Calvin would have agreed, about whether you could be Reformed and charismatic at the same time. How Bethan hated all these labels!

All Martyn had been trying to do was to find out what the Bible said. To him, a phrase like 'baptism in the Holy Spirit' wasn't what Pentecostals said it meant, or Calvinists, it was what the Bible said it was. But when he used the phrase in his sermons, people didn't listen to what he was actually saying at all!

Rather it was a case of some saying, 'Great! The Doctor agrees with us!' Or, 'Oh no! The Doctor has gone wrong! He's using that phrase. That group uses it all the time, and how

wrong they are. Now he's using it too, so he must be wrong...'
So again Martyn became a football in the argument between
the two sides.

As we in the family came to see, the combatants were
doing exactly what Martyn was saying to the Friday nighters
was so wrong: elevating the words of mere men to almost
biblical status. (Although I agreed with my grandfather on
all this, not all in the family did so. What we did all agree
on was what he had actually said, whether we agreed with
him or not!)

We all want our heroes to be 100% right - and to agree
with us! We all too often project what are actually our own
opinions back onto our hero. Then we can bask in the glory of
following someone so important. As you can see, this ends up
being a rather circular way of arguing.

So those Christians who wanted to have the respectability
of the great Dr. Lloyd-Jones agreeing with them were thrilled
when it looked as if Martyn was now on their side after all.
By contrast, those who had wanted to use his respectability
against such people were horrified when it came out in print
that Martyn did not agree with them on this issue at all.
(I emphasise in print because anyone who had heard those
sermons twenty years earlier would have known exactly what
he thought.) This comes onto another problem we have with
our heroes: we want them to be in 100% agreement with us,
not 90% or 80%.

We seem incapable of saying, 'Well, I agree with him on A,
B, C and D, but differ with him on E.' Or something like, 'His
view of Z is total rubbish, but I agree with him more than fully
on W, X and Y.' So people who agreed with him enthusiastically
on his wonderful rediscovery of the biblical doctrines of God's
grace to us in becoming Christians were horrified when he saw

in the Bible other doctrines, equally clearly taught in Scripture in his view, but on which both they and Calvin had a radically different interpretation. It was as if they couldn't bear him to be wrong! Which was why they felt his sermons, though thousands of people had heard them at the time, should be suppressed and never printed.

However, others felt that there was such a muddle on what he did or didn't say that the sermons ought to be printed, so that people could decide for themselves.

This was what Martyn would have wanted: for people to listen to his interpretation, to ponder it , then go back to the Bible and decide for themselves what was right. Whether he was right or not was not, ultimately, the issue, but what Scripture taught.

Not only that, but did your view make you alive in your Christian life? Did it give you zeal for the Lord, a yearning for the spiritual, a longing to follow Jesus more closely? For even if you were filled with zeal and a yearning for true doctrine simultaneously, that was what mattered. Doctrine isn't a set of head knowledge. Doctrine is the way in which we know how to know Jesus better. As a Romanian Christian once said, 'We may know a lot about Jesus, but do we know Jesus himself?'

It isn't a question of doctrine against experience, as seems to be the case in all too many churches, but doctrine with experience, experiencing the truth, life because of the truth that has happened within us.

This is why the row was such a shame, with so many people missing the point altogether. Doctrine without experience can be dry and arid. Experience without doctrine can lead into dangerous doctrinal error. We need, as did the Christians in the first century, to have not either or, but both.

I haven't gone into great depth on what Martyn actually said in *Joy Unspeakable*. Firstly, this is because you should read his sermons (and those in the new volume) for yourself. Then read Scripture to see whether or not you agree with him.

Secondly, I've tried in this chapter to lay out some principles instead:

How do we think as Christians?

What is really important?

This was something Martyn did with me and his other teenage grandchildren when he was alive. Learn the principles of thinking biblically now, and you can be set for life. It is what he wanted for the people of Westminster Chapel, for the millions worldwide who read his books, for you. It is what all Christians should wish for each other, since it is why God gave us his Word, the Bible, in the first place.

Hot for God

'Cool!' Everything seems to be 'cool' these days - the word is as popular among today's teens as it was in my teens in the late sixties.

Even a good essay on the foreign policy of King Henry VIII is 'cool', along with your favourite rock group or film. Yet being 'cool' or 'lukewarm' makes the Bible uneasy reading.

Words like 'zeal' and 'fire' go together uneasily with the whole idea behind 'cool'. Enthusiasm and displaying enthusiasm publicly is today, well, a little embarrassing, especially if it is a very open display by one of your parents in front of your friends. Jesus, though, gave his life for us, to redeem us. That, the Bible seems to argue, is hardly something to be cool about! Rather, our response should be one of endless enthusiasm, gratitude and praise - even eternity in Heaven will be too short a time to express properly all we owe to God for our salvation.

Cool isn't a new idea, to do with the Beatles or the Spice Girls. It actually goes back a long way, even back to the eighteenth century. Religion, said the fashionable trend setters of those days, was decidedly not something to take too seriously. They especially despised what they called 'enthusiasm', or, as we would put it today, any kind of 'uncool' behaviour.

Martyn Lloyd-Jones, often referred to himself as an 'eighteenth-century man'. By this he meant not that he was a follower of the fashion conscious eighteenth-century version of 'cool', but of the 'enthusiasts'. He once owned a picture of his great eighteenth-century enthusiastic hero, George Whitefield, who was preaching with tremendous enthusiasm to a crowd of very uncool, ordinary, mainly working class people. Martyn's one television programme, *The Awakener*, was on this extraordinary man, George Whitefield, and his times. (You can still get the video.) Whitefield was a personality who, like Martyn, had as much spiritual impact in America as in his native Britain.

The spiritual giants of the eighteenth-century, for example, George Whitefield, John Wesley and Charles Wesley (whose hymns we still sing), Daniel Rowlands (who like Martyn was from Llangeitho in Wales) and Jonathan Edwards in America - all deeply influenced Martyn.

However, as we've seen, Martyn agreed with them because he was convinced they had interpreted the Bible properly, not because they were great men. They were people who were alive and openly on fire for God in an age when enthusiasm of any kind was distinctly and often outrageously uncool.

These men didn't always agree with each other. The Wesley brothers, who founded Methodism, held some views which Whitefield and Edwards, for example, felt went a little astray in some areas. But they all had a passionate love for the Good News of Jesus, which they proclaimed wherever they went. Look at a hymn like Charles Wesley's *And Can It Be* and you can get an idea of how exciting they felt it was both to be a Christian and to share the Gospel.

Like Martyn, what these people had in common was the way in which they combined both doctrine and experience. They were graduates of the best universities, Oxford University in England and Yale in America, for example. Yet they had a passion which contrasted strongly with the rather dry 'cool' of their contemporaries, for whom the Christian faith was a mere intellectual curiosity and formal observance. Passionate intellectuals? Clever enthusiasts? Men like George Whitefield and Jonathan Edwards could easily hold their own with the greatest minds of their day, as Martyn was easily able to do with the cleverest professors of his own. Yet they could preach in a language that reached out to coal miners, factory girls, illiterate farm labourers, servants and outcasts, with thousands converted to a living faith in Jesus Christ. Indeed so many people were converted at this time that in Britain the time came to be called 'the Methodist Revival' and in America 'the Great Awakening'.

Martyn loved few things more than to read of revivals, which, in British English, mean times of special blessing from God, in which Christians have their lives transformed and scores of non-Christians are converted. Bethan had seen the Welsh Revival of 1904-5. Martyn had seen, especially in Wales from 1929-31, some quite remarkable things in his own ministry. He preached on revival at Westminster Chapel (you can read his book, *Revival*, on the subject) and lectured on it frequently. Sadly for him, he did not see further dramatic revival in Britain in his own lifetime, much though he longed and prayed for it. But the wonderful way in which God works at such times never ceased to fascinate him. One of the places at which he often used to lecture on revival was at the 'Puritan Conference' (or 'Westminster Conference', as it is known today). The seeds of this began with some student friends of Elizabeth's, back when she was at Oxford in the 1940s.

College food in those days was probably as stodgy as many school meals are today. So Elizabeth and her friends, Jim and Raymond, used to eat out sometimes at a very cheap eating place called The British Restaurant.

'I've found a great set of old books by someone who was here at Oxford over 300 years ago,' said Jim, a student with a keen mind and strong West Country burr. 'It may be really old, but it's so exciting!' he enthused. 'People then were the same as we are now: The same worries, fears, hopes. For example,' said

Jim, 'take the endless struggle that we all have, being tempted to do things that we know we shouldn't do, and not to do what we ought to do.'

Sound familiar? Well, these peopl,e like John Owen in the seventeenth-century, knew all about that. They even wrote about their own struggles with sin! They may have called such struggles the problem of 'indwelling sin' and similar phrases that we don't use today. These people were called the 'Puritans'. We sometimes think of them as dour and joyless, but such a caricature could not be further from the truth. The Puritans, Martyn would tell Elizabeth and her teenage friends, were realists.

'They knew all about life, about experience, or what they called experimental Christianity,' he said to them, after discovering that they had come to share his interest in the Puritans. 'Look at the great Christian classic, *Pilgrim's Progress*, by John Bunyan. Today we read it as literature, but it is a wonderful picture of all the struggles that we go through in our everyday Christian lives. We've all been there, even though we use our own words to describe the same experiences.' Many other Christians were, thanks to Martyn and, increasingly also to Elizabeth's friend, Jim Packer, discovering the Puritans and the amazing way in which people who lived 300 years ago had such deep, exciting relevance to us now. (See J. I. Packer's great classic, *Knowing God*, which I read as a teenager, and which is still in print, a book which, like Martyn's classic, *Spiritual Depression*, has helped millions of ordinary Christians world wide.)

'The Puritans were realistic,' Martyn would explain, 'just as the Bible is realistic. They knew, as people in the Bible did, that the Christian life is often a hard struggle.'

Read Martyn's *Spiritual Depression: Its Causes and Cures* and you can see how his medical knowledge of psychology and his

Puritan understanding of spiritual struggle combine to give a very special insight into the ups and downs of daily Christian life. Be encouraged! How often have you felt that no-one has a problem quite like you?

'I feel so alone,' you say. Isn't it wonderful to discover that many people know exactly how you feel, because they've been there too? Suddenly you aren't alone any more!

'That is why those seventeenth-century Puritans and the Christians who followed them in the eighteenth-century are so important for us,' Martyn would say, 'because they help us to see that all we struggle with today is just an updated twentieth-century version of exactly the same things they wrestled with back then. Technology might change, with cars, computers and aeroplanes, but human nature is just the same! In the twentieth-century, the seventeenth-century and right back in Bible times, we all go through the same things!'

Some people, though, got so excited by the Puritans that they started to use Puritan, seventeenth-century language. You may have heard enthusiastic but misguided preachers do the same today.

'They mean well, but miss the point,' Martyn would tell Jim and his other teenage enthusiasts. 'They're just what I would call good students - able to learn what people said in the past but unable to translate the same exciting, liberating truths into the language that ordinary Christians can speak today.' Martyn always spoke in a way in which people of his own time could understand. So too did the Puritans. They used the language of their time. They didn't use Chaucerian, fourteenth-century English! They were seventeenth-century people using seventeenth-century language.

But the feelings and emotions which they expressed are those equally relevant to first-century, thirteenth-century and twentieth-century people, like you or me. How often have you been to an older Christian, and said, 'I'm having a real trouble with problem A,' whatever that problem or struggle might be, only for them to reply,

'Disgusting! How can you think such wicked thoughts?' Not a very helpful response, is it? Now the Puritans, and their eighteenth-century followers would have understood you completely!

Just look at the Bible, which says that Jesus was tempted in all points just like we are. Everything! Every troubling thought you've had - Jesus was tempted ahead of you! Furthermore, as Martyn would point out, the Bible is filled with stories of God's people wrestling with this and that. The Bible makes it clear that we are in a state of permanent warfare with the Devil, who wants to make our spiritual lives as difficult and as miserable as possible. (*Spiritual Depression* deals with this in detail, as do Martyn's other books *The Christian Soldier* and *Christian Warfare*.) As Christians, we are in a state of lifelong warfare which does not end, until we die. But as Paul shows in the wonderful picture of the Christian soldier in his letter to the Ephesians, God does not leave us helpless. We have the Holy Spirit within us, the Bible to guide us and the spiritual armour with which to defend ourselves. This, as Martyn would point out, is a much more realistic picture of the Christian life than the one that some would have us believe. It is much more honest, too, than those misguided evangelists who say, 'Come to Jesus and all your problems will be solved.' The ultimate problem of our relationship to God, is of course solved when we become Christians! But at the same time, the moment we are converted, we are joining God's army, and becoming Satan's enemy! We will have spiritual struggles and battles the like of which we could not possibly have imagined.

As we saw, with Martyn having trained as a doctor, then having worked as a minister in a rough part of Wales during the Depression of the 1930s, nothing could shock him much. As we will see, he was the kindest, most patient and superbly understanding grandfather possible!

As a teenager, when I went to see him with a problem, worry, or troublesome thought, he would never say,

'How disgusting! Stop thinking such things at once!' He would rather recognise something which the Bible teaches, which the Puritans fully understood, but which we often forget today.

'You see,' he would explain, always calmly and lovingly, giving you his fullest attention as he did so, 'such unpleasant thoughts aren't really your own, even though they might appear to you as coming from inside you. They are the Devil, attacking you, trying either to get you to disobey God, or to make you so miserable, so wretched feeling, that you feel paralysed, unable to live the kind of Christian life that you'd like to. It isn't a sin to be tempted, or to be attacked spiritually by the Devil. But it is a sin to give in to temptation or to let the Devil paralyse you into inaction.' He would then explain how to deal with temptation, how to combat what the Bible calls 'the wiles of the Devil', whom the Apostle James in his letter to us describes as a roaring lion waiting to see who he can devour!

So when Puritans wrote great classics, such as *The Christian in Complete Armour,* they were writing about real life! Martyn, because he loved stories of revival, had a personal preference for the giants of the eighteenth-century. But he had a deep lifelong admiration for the Puritans of the sixteenth and seventeenth-centuries as well. For doctrine is never boring - not if it is taught and applied properly! That is something that Martyn always strove to do, whether preaching to thousands every Sunday, adapting sermons into books to be read by millions, or speaking one to one in private to ordinary

Christians about life's everyday struggles. Our Christian faith is always relevant, and God's guide to us, the bible, therefore is equally relevant for us now.

As Martyn showed us, we shouldn't look to great Christians of the past to guide us instead of the Bible. But their writing, their struggles, their insights can help us to see things in the Bible that we might otherwise have missed. Their mistakes can help us to avoid similar mistakes today. We can learn from them to avoid becoming too dry or too over enthusiastic about one doctrine at the expense of others. Their example in being 'hot' Christians, hot for God and for his Good News, hot for living the kind of Christian lives that God wants us to live, can encourage us now. People in their own day wanted to be 'cool', to be fashionable, to be like everyone else, and not stand out as being different. They know how hard it was to be against the flow - more than we do today in fact, because while we might be laughed at for being 'keen', 'religious', 'boring', many Puritans were sent to prison for their beliefs. This is a fate far worse than anything we have to suffer today.

So when people laughed at Martyn or scoffed at his ideas he knew, as we can, that there were Christians who had gone through hard times long before he had. Above all, those Puritans, those eighteenth-century followers, knew how exciting Christian faith could be! It wasn't surprising really that they were enthusiastic: they had the most exciting thing of all to be excited about: new life in Jesus Christ!

As a Welshman, Martyn didn't have problems with emotion that cooler Anglo-Saxons (English and many Americans) have, although he knew the dangers of emotional excess for its own sake too. But the Puritans and Methodists were often English! No stiff upper lips for them! Christianity was an experience of the very highest kind possible!

Some of you come from churches with lots of emotion. How much solid Bible teaching do you have? Do you find yourself thinking that the Bible and doctrine are boring? How can something so exciting possibly be dull? Some of you come from churches that are very 'sound', with long sermons and correct doctrine. But how much experience is there in your church - of a biblical kind? How much 'zeal for the Lord', as the Puritans would say, is there?

'Theology,' as Martyn once described preaching, 'comes through a man who is on fire.' Head and heart, heart and head - we were given both by God, not one or the other! That is the great gift from God that Martyn rediscovered, in the Bible, in the writings and in the lives of the Puritans and from the giants of the eighteenth-century awakenings.

What is really exciting and a challenge to us in the self-consciously 'cool' age in which we live, is that we can live such Christian lives too. 'Cool!' or 'Hot!' It's a choice we each have to make. Let the flame of the Spirit of Jesus keep your faith ablaze: a fire that will never go out!

Thinking Further Topics

Fire in Llangeitho

Martyn's was quite an extraordinary life, as I trust you will agree. Martyn regarded teenagers as intelligent people in their own right, not simply as the children of their parents. He was a great encourager. One of the things that he encouraged teenagers to do was to work things out for themselves, to come to their own conclusions. Just because you're born of Christian parents, for example, doesn't mean that you're a Christian yourself.

Martyn's parents were church goers. In those days, most people went to church, although even then the numbers were going down rapidly. So, does coming from a Christian home make you a Christian? Does belonging to a church going family make you a Christian? What makes anyone a Christian? Perhaps you've never really thought about what being a Christian really is? Why not take an easy version of the Bible that doesn't have the off-putting language of some versions, and read one of the Gospels for yourself? (Two versions which you could try are the *New International Version* or the *Contemporary English Version*. You could go to your local Christian bookshop and ask for advice.)

Think about what makes you a Christian? Find out what Jesus says about that in his word. How do you measure up beside Jesus Christ's criteria? Are you a Christian in your own right? Or is your Christian faith just something second-hand from other people?

Think hard and find out.

Early Days

What have the key influences in your life been up to now? What has made you what you are today? All of us come from very different backgrounds. Martyn came from his, I from mine, you from yours. Look at your parents. Maybe each of them had very different backgrounds. Martyn Lloyd-Jones was not a wealthy man. His daughter (my mother) was brought up with very little money. My father, however, was raised in a very privileged family, where money was seldom a problem. All these things shape us in many ways. How much of your life do you take for granted? Has it shaped you for good? Or have there been things that, if you ponder them, have been unhelpful? What things have helped you to know God better? Do you really believe that things 'just happen' to you? Or does God have a say in it all? Can you look back and say,

'Well, that wasn't so great, but God really taught me something there'? Or - 'This is wonderful! I must always remember to thank God for what he gives me and does for me.'

Look at letters like those of Paul to Timothy and see how God shapes our lives in the directions that he wants.

Martyn: The Bart's Man

What do you want to be? Perhaps I should rephrase that. 'Why do you want to be what you want to be?' Is it something that God wants us to be? Are we in it for money? To impress people? Even the so-called 'caring' professions can be entered for wrong reasons. 'Isn't she wonderful? She's a nurse . . .' 'It must be great to be a missionary.' Yes, we can even become full-time Christian workers with half an eye on the praise that we will get from other Christians.

Many of you may be going straight from school into a job. Those going to college or university may choose a subject that can lead to a chosen career.

So: what motivates you? How compatible is that with your Christian faith? There's nothing wrong with a high salary - we need Christians in the business community, for example, bringing Christian standards to the factory floor or management team. But what are our motives? Even in lower paid jobs, we can get eaten up with the promotion rat race, putting other things before God.

Christian work is no exception: Martyn Lloyd-Jones' daughter once wrote of the 'Evangelical widow syndrome'. This was when people spent so much time on church work that they neglected spouses and children. Remember: it is God we are to obey and please, not people, friends, or family. How are you managing? For it is often in our teens that we make the decisions that will determine the rest of our lives. What you decide today can affect your future!

Love in London

Maybe you are dating at the moment, or hoping to meet someone! What sort of things are you looking for? Someone with fabulous looks? Someone who'll make you look good in front of other people? Someone you get on well with? Someone whose interests you share? Someone who shares your Christian faith? Someone who makes you think about why you believe as you do?

Lots of helpful books have been written for teenagers on the issue of sex, so I won't add to all that here. Rather, I want to ask: If you want to get married, what things are important to you - and why? It is too easy to go with the crowd on these kinds of issues. Dating is one of the most difficult areas of life by far in which to be a Christian and to appear different from everyone else. Christians can also give the impression of being wimpish or unattractive because they have different values and attitudes.

Of course we must make sure that it is our Christianity people dislike us for, not our personal hygiene! It is a challenge to be loving and caring as Christians and not arrogant in defence of our views. It is often a struggle to be a Christian when it comes to love and romance. God asks us to act in certain ways not because he is a hard-nosed heavenly dictator, but because he always wants the best for us.

Try to avoid the mentality of one missionary who gave a talk when I was a teenager. This person was involved in beach evangelism and said, 'Many young people go off on beach holidays. The good looking ones find someone and we talk to the ones who get left behind.'

Good grief! If you look at Peter's letters, he makes clear: a) that Christians can have a hard time for being different, b) that when it comes to things such as outward appearance, Christians shouldn't give undue attention to these matters. He even discusses hairstyles: human nature is no different 2000 years later from what it was then! Rather, he says, it is the inward person that lasts. Bethan Phillips as a teenager was beautiful and fashionable. Eighty years later, such things had long since faded. But the personality was greatly improved by eighty years of Christian living!

Martyn met his wife in church. I also met my wife in church seventy-six years later - it seems a good place! Martyn and Bethan had fifty-four years of happy married life, with their Christian faith very much in common. It took Bethan twelve years to realise that Martyn had the qualities she needed as a husband, even though he wasn't ever fashionable or in her league of looks. They had differing qualities and each complemented the other person. You don't have to be the same to be happy!

Above all, though, they were both devoted to the same Christian message, to Christian values, to thinking spiritually. Is this what you are looking for? Something much deeper than outward appearance, something that is permanent and which will last you a lifetime? If you are, then you are looking for the very thing God wants for you: to be more like Christ.

Wales' New Doctor of the Heart

Martyn gave up fame and fortune, to work for far less money with the poor and underprivileged. But this had an ironic outcome: through his preaching and writing he didn't end up rich, but he did become world famous! What are our priorities? What do we want out of life? Perhaps an important question to ask is: Do we truly trust God to keep us going through what we believe he wants us to do?

When Martyn gave up the bright London lights, the high society connections, and the prospect of an outstanding medical career he did not know that God would bless him with an international ministry that gave him influence far beyond anything he could ever have had as a top physician. All he knew was that God had called him to live and work in the slums of Aberavon. The fame he had later did not come straight away, either. It was not until he was well into his forties that he became the household name worldwide that he has been ever since. The very idea of achieving fame was quite alien to him anyway. What are you after? Fame? Fortune? Or do you want to do what God wants you to do?

You won't necessarily achieve fame as your reward either! Most of us have nowhere near the fame of a Martyn Lloyd-Jones or a Billy Graham. But we will be able to share with them the inner spiritual satisfaction of knowing that we are doing God's will.

Unspeakable Joy

The 'gifts of the Spirit' issue is, sadly, one of the most divisive in the Church today. For Christians to be against each other is very sad especially when we should be united on the key areas of the Gospel itself. Obviously then, I am not going to be able to solve the issue in these few paragraphs! Nor will you. Rather than give any definitive answers I am going to suggest some areas of possible study. First and foremost, read the Bible! Look at the book of Acts, where the 'gifts' first appear. Then read Paul's letters where he talks about them in some more detail (Romans 12, I Corinthians 12, Ephesians 4). Paul also discusses the 'baptism' or 'sealing' with the Holy Spirit in the Romans and Ephesians passages. What thoughts do you get from these references? What is Luke describing in Acts? What is Paul writing about in his letters? How do these two things relate to one another: a) the descriptive passages in Acts and b) the teaching passages in Paul's letters? Then read what Martyn wrote in his book, *Joy Unspeakable*.

If Martyn was in the room, what would you ask him? Where has he got it right? Would you disagree with him? Remember that you should base your conclusions on what you think the Bible is saying in relation to what he wrote. Don't say, 'Well, I think my minister would say X.' Remember, your pastor or vicar needs to defend everything he says from Scripture too! Why not read books from people who take opposite viewpoints on the subject? Go to your local Christian bookshop for advice on what books to read. Where are these authors right? Where are they wrong? Are their views always incompatible? For example,

I once knew of two churches, one that believed in miraculous healing and one that didn't. But the second church saw many healed, through 'answered prayer'. In reality, both believed the same things, but just described them differently! Lastly, is this an issue on which churches and Christians should divide? Can you be in the same church and/or have Christian fellowship with those who think differently to you? Is it like saying, 'Jesus never rose from the dead' Or rather like, 'Well, these Baptists baptise one way, and those Presbyterians and Anglicans another, but we're all Evangelicals.' What is really important: and what isn't?

What labels do you give yourself, and why? These are things to work out scripturally for yourself, and discuss with other Christians - your parents (if you're from a Christian home), a church leader, older Christians in your church. Think it through, reach your own conclusions. Don't try to split your church if your conclusion is different! But be sure that your conclusions are Bible-based. If they are real, from God, then your experience won't be like the kinds of 'high' which people at school may have. It will be something solid, lasting and improving. It will be from God and will make you more Christlike and more effective in your Christian walk and life. Whatever view we take on the gifts and baptism with the Holy Spirit, to be more Christlike is something upon which we can all agree.

Feeling Down?

How often we think that we're alone in facing our problems! No one has had it quite as bad as we have! Yet when we read the Bible, we discover that the great heroes of the faith were there before us. Elijah, after Mount Carmel, the disciples after the crucifixion, Timothy with his nerves - all these people went through hard times, too. Just look at the Psalms, especially one like Psalm 73 (about which Martyn wrote in his book, *Faith: Tried and Triumphant*).   Read the autobiographies of many leading Christians (especially the Puritans, who were so refreshingly honest) and you will discover that they went through all the ups and downs that we endure today. Read the Bible passages upon which Martyn based his book, *Spiritual Depression*, and then read the book itself. Don't many of the problems feel familiar? Yes, you've been there too! (Maybe you're there right now: the teens do seem to be the part of life where you can be open and honest about your ups and downs!)

The Bible is a very practical book. It is the book which is absolutely true to life. God made us - he inspired the Bible! It is not surprising really that God's word to us gives us the practical guide that we need to show us the way through the downs as well as the ups.

Look up the following verses. The Bible tells us a lot about how to feel and behave. Think about what these verses tell us about feeling down. Remind yourself the next time you suffer from the blues that God understands how we feel. Our behaviour upsets him sometimes. He is not a God that doesn't feel. After reading these verses it might be a good idea to sit down with your Bible and a concordance. This is an index of all the different themes and words in the Bbile. Go through the verses which deal with sorrow, sin and difficulties. Pray before you read the Bible that God will teach you from his word. Write down what you learn so that you can remember what God teaches you at a later date.

If you don't have a concordance go to your local Christian bookshop. They will be happy to recommend one to you.

VERSES

Psalm 16:4

Psalm 32:5

Psalm 38:18

Psalm 69:2

Psalm 130: 1

Psalm 116:3

Isaiah 35:10

Isaiah 53:3

Mark 14:34

2 Corinthians 7:10

2 Corinthians 6:10

Heaven

Being a teenager, there is a chance that you have both parents and maybe all four grandparents still alive. I had all four grandparents until I was nearly nineteen, and three alive until I was twenty-six. Maybe, though, bereavement is not at all unfamiliar to you - someone in your family, an old person at church, or even a friend may have died.

Three of my school friends died in a car crash in South America just after leaving school. The brother of a friend committed suicide. All these deaths happened in and around my teenage years.

When we are young, it is only natural to think that we're immortal! We have the whole of life ahead of us, and, statistically speaking, if we live in Western countries such as Britain or the USA, we probably do. Yet as Jesus reminds us in several parables, death comes like a thief in the night. We will probably live to at least 60 or 65. But we can't guarantee it! Furthermore, you might, like me, get hit by a severe illness that changes your plans, as happened to me in my late thirties. This might force you to make unexpected changes. (I got better, by the way, but I've had friends who haven't.)

Death forces us to face up to ultimate realities: we might be able to get lawyers smart enough to help us avoid taxes, but nothing can help us to avoid death! It's coming! If you know people who have died, how did you react? How did other people you know take the death? Was the person who died a Christian? Were their friends and family Christian? A friend of mine, not much older than me, died not so long ago, leaving a widow in her early thirties with two small children. It was a tragedy for those remaining that he had died so young. But while we were all sad, especially his family, we knew, as they did, that Graham was now in heaven.

As I write this, the father of someone at my church has just died. He was in his eighties, a more suitable age perhaps, but no less sad for his daughter. The elderly man's funeral was a celebration of a life lived in Christ. Graham's funeral, even though his death was premature, was the same. For Christians, death is no longer the final enemy.

How do you face issues like death? What matters most to you? What are the ultimate realities in your life? For in Christ we have life eternal! Is that true for you? I pray that it will be and for all those who read this book. Martyn would not have wanted it to be any other way!

'Death where is your sting. Grave where is your victory.'
1 Corinthians 15:55

Other publications
mentioned in this book

A Family Portrait Christopher Catherwood, Kingsway.
Five Evangelicals Christopher Catherwood,
Christian Focus Publications.
Knowing God by J. Packer, Hodder & Stoughton
Passion for Holiness by J.Packer, Kingsway.
Among God's Giants by J. Packer, Kingsway.
A Quest for Holiness by J. Packer, Crossway.
Life in the Spirit, in Marriage, Home and Work
by Martyn Lloyd-Jones, Banner of Truth.
Joy Unspeakable by Martyn Lloyd-Jones, Kingsway
Spiritual Depression
by Martyn Lloyd-Jones, OM Books
The Christian Soldier
by Martyn Lloyd-Jones, Banner of Truth
Christian Warfare
by Martyn Lloyd-Jones, Banner of Truth
Faith: Tried and Triumphant
by Martyn Lloyd-Jones, IVP
The Christian in Complete Armour
by William Gurnell, Banner of Truth
Pilgrims Progress by John Bunyan

LIGHTKEEPERS

Ten boys who made a Difference
ISBN 1 85792 7753
Ten girls who made a Difference
ISBN 1 85792 7761
Ten boys who didn't Give In
ISBN 1 84550 0350

The Lightkeepers series by Irene Howat is an excellent collection of short biographies on famous and dynamic Christians from history and the present day. Fact files, prayers and quizzes will make these books favourites for years to come.

Look out for characters such as Augustine; Monica of Hippo; Polycarp and Alban - all characters influential in the early church. As well as people like Joni Eareckson Tada, Corrie Ten Boom and Martin Luther.

Other titles in this series are:
Ten boys who Changed the World;
Ten girls who Changed the World;
Ten boys who made History;
Ten girls who made History;
Ten girls who didn't Give In.

TRAILBLAZERS

John Newton:
A Slave Set Free
ISBN 1 85792 8342

Robert Murray McCheyne:
Life is An Adventure
ISBN 1 85792 9470

Richard Wurmbrand:
A Voice in the Dark
ISBN 1 85792 2980

The Trailblazers series are an excellent series of books to give good role models to young people. Throughout history God has chosen men to be strong and steadfast witnesses to his glory. Christians have been in the forefront of new ideas and adventures; travel and social justice as well as struggling against dictatorships and persecution.

The Trailblazer series gives children a good selection of men and women from the past and the present who not only show us how to live our lives on earth but also bring us closer to our Heavenly Father.

TRAILBLAZERS

Mary Slessor:
Servant to the Slave
ISBN 1 85792 3480

Corrie ten Boom:
The Watchmaker's Daughter
ISBN 1 85792 116X

Joni Eareckson Tada:
Swimming Against the Tide
ISBN 1 85792 8334

As well as providing excellent role models for young boys, the Trailblazer series provides heroines for young girls as well. Throughout history God has chosen women to be pioneers and defenders of the faith. As Christians they have travelled to countries that many men feared to step in. Their untiring work for social justice as well as their struggles for freedom and equality are examples to us all.

The Trailblazer series gives children a good selection of men and women from the past and the present who not only show us how to live our lives on earth but also bring us closer to our Heavenly Father.

TORCHBEARERS

Polycarp waited until the sound of marching footsteps faded away. The Praetorian guard were on the move – ready to pounce on Christians or any other 'revolutionaries' that they might find.

These are the days when the catacombs are the dark shadowy refuges of the Christians and the amphitheatre is the sound of death to the believer. Polycarp will be one of the church leaders called on to give his life for Christ and his Kingdom... and this is something he counts as an honour.

To gain the Crown of Fire he must be willing to suffer for Christ. But will his courage hold? Accompany Polycarp and his companions as they face up to the Roman enemy and pass on the legacy of truth. The golden chain around Polycarp's neck is a link to the past in more ways than one.

William Chad Newsom is a new writer with a flare for the dramatic. Included in the book are a time line and further facts about the early church.

ISBN: 1 84550 0415

Staying Faithful - Reaching Out!

Christian Focus Publications publishes books for adults and children under its three main imprints: Christian Focus, Mentor and Christian Heritage. Our books reflect that God's word is reliable and Jesus is the way to know him, and live for ever with him.

Our children's publication list includes a Sunday school curriculum that covers pre-school to early teens; puzzle and activity books. We also publish personal and family devotional titles, biographies and inspirational stories that children will love.

If you are looking for quality Bible teaching for children then we have an excellent range of Bible story and age specific theological books.

From pre-school to teenage fiction, we have it covered!

Find us at our web page:
www.christianfocus.com